"In his brilliant book, Finnian shines a spotlight on an issue that I and so many others have dealt with; so many of us are surviving and not actually *living* a life. It's through not only his meticulous research, but also his inner journey, that we are offered a path toward *feeling* the way most of us have assumed is unattainable."

— **Wesley Schultz**, *of The Lumineers*

"Finnian is the perfect guide to transform your life and optimize your sense of purpose and fulfillment. As a professional athlete, I know firsthand how important breath is to high performance in all elements of life. Finnian's work creates an approachable on-ramp for anyone wishing to design their life to feel their absolute best. *Intentionality* is a game changer."

— **Colin O'Brady**, *10-time world record–holding explorer and* New York Times *best-selling author of* The Impossible First

"*Intentionality* provides a fresh perspective by merging ancient wisdom with a comprehensive road map for transformation. Finnian artfully brings us back to the present to experience all of what life has to offer."

— **Maya Marcia Wieder**, *CEO of Dream University and best-selling author of* Dream

"Through raw honesty and compelling storytelling, Finnian invites you to reconsider what it truly means to live with intention and from a place of feeling. I believe leaders would greatly benefit from applying his methodology within their organizations to create a high-performing culture and ignite sustainable growth."

— **Ron "Omani" Carson**, *co-author of* The Sustainable Edge *and founder and chairman of Carson Wealth*

INTENTI●NALITY

INTENTI●NALITY

A Groundbreaking Guide to Breath, Consciousness, and Radical Self-Transformation

FINNIAN KELLY

HAY HOUSE LLC
Carlsbad, California • New York City
London • Sydney • New Delhi

Published in the United States by: Hay House LLC: www.hayhouse.com®
Published in Australia by: Hay House Australia Publishing Pty Ltd: www.hayhouse.com.au
Published in the United Kingdom by: Hay House UK Ltd: www.hayhouse.co.uk
Published in India by: Hay House Publishers (India) Pvt Ltd: www.hayhouse.co.in

Cover design by Faceout Studio, Jeff Miller
Interior design: Karim J. Garcia

Cataloging-in-Publication Data is on file at the Library of Congress

Hardcover ISBN: 978-1-4019-7754-2
E-book ISBN: 978-1-4019-7762-7
Audiobook ISBN: 978-1-4019-7763-4

10 9 8 7 6 5 4 3 2 1
1st edition, June 2024

Printed in the United States of America

SUSTAINABLE
FORESTRY
INITIATIVE

Certified Chain of Custody
Promoting Sustainable Forestry
www.forests.org
SFI-01268

SFI label applies to the text stock

If you want to awaken all of humanity, then awaken all of yourself. If you want to eliminate the suffering in the world, then eliminate all that is dark and negative in yourself. Truly, the greatest gift you have to give is that of your own self-transformation.

— **LAO-TZU**

To my next spiritual teacher, Ossian Bear Kelly.
I made a promise to myself as a little boy that I would
show you the love that I wished I could have felt.
This book was my personal journey to get to a place
where I was ready to honor this promise.
I love being on this trip with you.
Thank you for making my miracle.

CONTENTS

INTRODUCTION

Why Intentionality?

Seven years ago, I woke up blindsided by my own naivete.

I had what I thought was my best life—what I truly believed was a meticulously crafted, intentional life. I was living in a mansion in Beaver Creek, Colorado, and skiing 100 days of the year. I had financial independence after exiting a company and was married to a woman I loved.

But soon enough, the dream I'd worked so hard for snowballed into my worst nightmare. A couple months before our wedding, the father of my then fiancée, Sarah, died unexpectedly after falling down the stairs. This was a man I'd just started to accept as the only real father figure in my adult life—and then he was gone.

Following the wedding, things continued to spiral. We'd just sold a business. We thought we'd make a lot of money and followed through on our plan to move from Australia to Colorado to enjoy the "rich" life. But after finding ourselves in a legal battle with Sarah's father's estate and selling the company to what turned out to be bad-faith buyers, the mental and financial challenges began mounting.

We were grieving and burned out, and our relationship was deteriorating faster than either of us realized at the time.

Then one day, a year after our move to America, Sarah left. And just like that, our marriage was over.

The end of our marriage was my rock bottom in business and in life. It was the most alone, depleted, and trapped I'd ever felt.

There were days when I was holding on for dear life—and it felt easier to dilute my self-worth rather than fight for it. There were days when I clung to regret from my past—because at the time, the past was the only thing I could come to terms with. The thoughts of my present and future were far too heavy.

Nothing was working. I woke up one day and said, "I don't ever want to feel like this again." What I wasn't fully aware of at the time was a very fine distinction in the language. I didn't say, "I don't ever want to *think* this way again." I said, "I don't ever want to *feel* this way again."

And that's when the light bulb came on.

When my marriage unraveled, this question of "What do I want?" popped up again. Based on what I'd been taught to believe and to think, and how I'd been taught to behave and to feel, I'd designed what I thought was my perfect life. I acted the way the people around me wanted me to act. I was educated. I served in the armed forces. I was financially independent and could afford nice things. By all accounts, I was living with great intention. But once I had achieved the vision for my life, the illusion came crashing down.

That's when I realized I needed a new approach—one that was less binary and more of a merging of mindsets that accurately represented the full spectrum of my background and beliefs. I had clouded ideologies around masculinity and was checking the boxes of what I was supposed to be doing as a man and a husband. I was viewing life through the lens of *when* instead of *why*—meaning that I always thought in loaded terms like, "When this happens, our marriage will be better," instead of "Why? Why do we believe this will make our marriage last?" Or, "Why do we believe these things will make us happy or whole?"

So, in preparation for my newly single life, I started soul-searching. I thought about what my new approach would have to entail, and I was reminded of a friend who'd once nicknamed me "the Business Mystic." He was describing the distinct intersection of my entrepreneurial drive and my spiritual nature. I had a master's of science degree in positive psychology and a bachelor's degree in mathematics and physics. I'd also taken on numerous leadership roles in the past decade of my involvement in the Entrepreneurs' Organization's global network. I'd built and sold multiple million-dollar companies. And yet there was also a side of me that felt drawn to the spiritual world, and there were things I had a great deal of faith in but could not wrap my head around: they were rooted in a feeling.

In a world where so much of our personal and professional identities are often boxed into a single specialty or identity, I felt seen in my friend's description. I felt like he had understood me. And I wanted to explore further alongside the scientists, thought leaders, philosophers, and spiritual teachers who shared my desire to find the commonalities in the scientific and spiritual communities rather than the chasms between them. This, I thought, is where I could find my way.

It was then that I read the Quran, the Bible, the Bhagavad Gita, the Dhammapada, the Tao Te Ching, and more. I combed through Einstein's findings and the work of David Bohm and David Hawkins. I read Carl Sagan, who, for me, had nailed it when he wrote, "Science is not only compatible with spirituality; it is a profound source of spirituality."[1]

I'd found some spiritual communities whom I really connected with, but unfortunately much of the landscape had become flooded with people who talked about spirituality as if it were something to be conquered or completed. And in the scientific world, I came across people I held in great regard but who rejected anything that couldn't be proven with numbers, data, or anything physically quantifiable. Thus far, my life experience had really only been framed through the latter primitive perspective—one that anointed the more masculine, logical reasoning and often dismissed the more feminine or emotional angles.

And the reality is, it just wasn't enough of a life of meaning. Not for me. And my readings revealed why. They reminded me that everything I'd worked for had come from living in survival mode instead of living with intention. I feared disappointing others and myself. I was confusing being disciplined with being rigid. I struggled to stay in the present, and I constantly compared what I had to what others had. Speaking of what I had, I always believed there was never enough time or energy in the day. And I could not, no matter what I did, stop focusing on long-term plans and stories—which left me very little to enjoy or experience along the way.

Every single aspect of my life and my behavior had become an unfulfilling escapade in self-preservation. But what had I preserved? Not my marriage. Not my dignity. Certainly not my happiness, my purpose, or my passion.

I didn't want to live in survival mode. I didn't want to be consumed with self-preservation. What I wanted was inner peace. I just hadn't figured out how to truly capture it yet.

That's when I changed the question. I no longer asked, "What do I want?" Instead, I asked, "How do I want to feel?"

And once that light bulb was on, it stayed on. The pressure to think was off, and the incentive to feel was greater than ever before.

I carried that energy into my readings—of both scientific and spiritual texts—and found that both disciplines want to help us understand the nature of the universe and how we fit into it. One has a more internal-facing path, while the other proposes a more empirical methodology, but at their core, they embrace complex, imperfect explorations of the universal truths that make us human and connect us to something far bigger than ourselves. I also found what I identified as the five core priorities of a human being. I believed these priorities would help me find inner peace and, quite frankly, make life worth living.

So I decided to make these my own personal top five priorities—five ways of behaving that I could intentionally focus on that would be my compass on my path to inner peace. I wanted to *love* and to be loved. I wanted to *grow*, and I wanted to be a part of the growth in the people and world around me. I wanted to *serve*, to know that changes in me could positively change the lives of others. I wanted to *play*, to be lighthearted and childlike whenever I could do so. I wanted to *create*, to never lose the spark to build and make magic in my own life and beyond.

I knew in my heart that focusing on these priorities was how I was going to move myself out of my conditioned survival mode and to leave a life of self-preservation behind.

That's when the blueprint for Intentionality came to be.

For the first time, I let go of needing to control my future and instead focused on my feelings. I saw that this was clearly the only path that would lead to inner peace—and I truly believed I could change. Just as I believe in my heart that you can. It is my sincere hope that this book provides you with what I didn't know I deserved all those years ago. No more guessing what you want. No more illusions. With Intentionality, you don't have to choose between faith and facts. You can make your own miracles at the wellspring where they meet.

Intentionality will teach you—as it has taught me and count-less others—three definitive lessons:

First, you are born with the tools to build the life you're searching for. Every one of us has access to the same univer-sal support—and to our breath, our greatest technology and superpower!

Second, what you are searching for is a feeling. You've been taught that you should strive for outcomes—that when you achieve a certain goal or get a material object, you'll be ful-filled. You may feel satisfied for a brief moment, but it never lasts—because what you're actually in search of is a feeling. No one else knows the feeling you're searching for. You have to dis-cover it for yourself and then shape your life to experience it.

Third, you always have a choice. We all have agency, and the sooner you can acknowledge that you have contributed—whether subconsciously or consciously—to every circumstance in your life, the better. This acknowledgment will likely cause friction within you, and if this is the case, it's okay. You will come to realize that choice can liberate you and empower you to take radical responsibility for your life.

In an effort to share with you these three lessons, and ensure you are equipped and inspired to choose your own path for a more intentional way of life, I have divided this book into five parts:

Part I: Your System. Within you is an intricate, interconnected system composed of your breath, your multilayered mind, and your energy centers. Here you will explore the different roles each plays, how they work in tandem, and what physiological and psychological effects they are capable of delivering.

Part II: Your Coding. Your subconscious mind is made up of countless impressions that have taken root from the earliest moments of your life. From family, to language, to media consumption and more, in this section you will dive into the external influences that shape how you experience the world and inspire the need for more consciousness. You'll also learn the impact the ego has in driving your thoughts and behaviors.

Part III: Recoding. At the heart of your subconscious are deeply ingrained belief loops. Fortunately, they are malleable. In this portion of the book, you will tap into a detailed study of two of the driving forces behind Intentionality—repetition and energy interventions.

Part IV: Behaviors and Tools. Maintaining the benefits of positive belief loop creation and staying on your path requires consistency. Part IV provides you with the practical behaviors and tools that will be a daily reinforcement on your Intentionality journey.

Part V: Scientific Manifestation. While the preceding parts of the book will give you every reason to, as they say, "trust the process," the scientific manifestation process serves as the finale for a reason. In this last installment, you'll take a quantum leap to tangible progress in your Intentionality journey—one where you'll combine science and spirituality to clarify, conceive, and claim what you desire.

Somebody recently asked me how I would define spirituality . . . I've always said that spirituality couldn't exist without science and vice versa, and so I answered in a way that I believe takes the division out of the two approaches: "Spirituality is just getting to know yourself better." Because when you do, you will connect to something bigger than you.

This book will leave you with greater self-awareness and a deeper understanding of the role feeling plays in your system. You'll be able to rewire your circuitry and discover the best possible ways to implement Intentionality into the way you live and the way you lead.

And this book will embolden you to challenge your beliefs, because that is an imperative step in order to feel so you can heal, come full circle, and return to your true nature.

This book will also empower you to do what I did—to abandon a life spent in survival mode, embrace an existence that merges the power of science and spirituality, and experience the lasting radical transformation that comes with self-awareness.

And perhaps most importantly, this book will inspire you to take action, because reading on its own will not be enough. And because in its simplest terms, that's what Intentionality is—identifying how you want to feel and taking incremental steps toward that reality.

Part I

YOUR SYSTEM

Happy people build their inner world.
Unhappy people blame their outer world.

— **THE BUDDHA**

CHAPTER 1

BREATH

In addition to the five universal priorities at the core of some of the most famed spiritual texts I mentioned in the Introduction, a shared origin story of humanity also persists: that of the breath of life. While many truths have been corrupted by the individual and collective egos and have, at times, been used to create separation and divisions throughout history, the power of breath remains as a beacon for unity in body and spirit. In many languages, the word for *breath* is the same word used for *soul*, *life*, and *spirit* too. The English word *spirit* is derived from the Latin root *spir*, which means "breath."

In the Old Testament (Genesis 2:7), it is written, "Then the Lord God formed man of dust from the ground, and breathed into his nostrils the breath of life; and man became a living being." And Job 33:4 tells us, "The Spirit of God has made me, And the breath of the Almighty gives me life."

The New Testament (John 20:22) says, "And when he had said this, he breathed on them and said to them 'Receive the Holy Spirit.'"

Confucius said, "What has to be taught first is the breath."

The Quran (Surah Al-Hijr 15:29) offers, "So when I have proportioned him and breathed into him of My [created] soul, then fall down to him in prostration."

A Sanskrit proverb reminds us, "For breath is life, and if you breathe well, you will live long on earth."

And the Anapanasati Sutta, a 16-part set of Buddhist teachings around breath and mindfulness, implores us to remember that, "Mindfully breathing in, mindfully breathing out, one calm's one's bodily processes."

What these words underscore is that breath is the great connector. It reminds us that we are all breathing in the same air, even the air of those whom we may disagree with or whose common humanity we may have minimized or diminished. Breath is the beginning, the end, and the tether between us all. It's what keeps us alive. It's what gives us meaning. It's the one thing we can't live without for the shortest amount of time. It's the wiring between all living organisms that proves we're not separated or disconnected, but rather that we are being routed through the same network. It reveals that we are dependent on each other—that with every breath we take in and exhale, we become more firmly enmeshed in a larger system, one that reveals much more about our similarities than about our differences.

It is precisely this reason that breath is a core tenet of Intentionality. Intentionality is rooted in optimizing systems—both within you and the world around you.

The breath usually does not require our thoughts because it is regulated by the autonomic nervous system, also known as the involuntary nervous system, which controls automatic physiological processes like heart rate, blood pressure, and digestion. While these functions all happen automatically in the body, the breath is different because we can also consciously choose to control it, and this is what is meant by the term *breathwork*. The immune system, digestive system, brain, heart, and nervous system are all positively impacted by consciously controlled breathing.

Throughout this book, you can expect custom breathing exercises that embrace the intersection of science and spirituality, that help you settle into the subject at hand, and that empower you to make the necessary connections between breath and building the life you've been searching for. Think of these as the circuit breakers you might find in your home—the ones on the wall that allow for all your devices and power systems to run simultaneously and that also offer an instantly resettable fuse.

Essentially, circuit breakers allow for the safe functionality of everything in your environment. They're designed to stop your circuits from going into overload—which can include overheating, short-circuiting, burning out, and even catching on fire. When we talk about systems—and particularly about the loops and cycles within them that aren't working—a circuit breaker will serve as the mechanism for you to detect and halt any malfunctioning within your system and reset for what's next. It will help you navigate emotions and sensations in your body by equipping you to *respond* rather than *react* to that emotional trigger—enabling you to feel the emotion and let it flow through you. And last, but certainly not least, it will also help you reach a heightened spiritual experience within yourself.

So, what do I mean by "a heightened spiritual experience through breath"? And what does it look and feel like? Well, when you tap into your breath, into the one innate technology available to each and every one of us, you will be able to better interpret what is happening in your body. You will understand how to engage with your operating system. And you will be drawn to the world of possibilities that comes when you choose to focus on feelings rather than outcomes. It will stir you up, settle you down, and balance you out. And more than ever before, it will drive you to be firmly in the present moment.

So before you begin with the first circuit breaker, take a moment to look inward at your system as it currently stands. Try answering these questions: What's your breath like now? What sensations do you notice in your physical body? Do you have a lot of thoughts? What mood are you in, and how would you describe it?

And remember, don't overthink it. Dive right in—because this first circuit breaker's one and only job is to align your mind, heart, and body for an all-encompassing experience of Intentionality.

Circuit Breaker:
Heart Coherence Breath

According to the HeartMath Institute, "because breathing patterns modulate the heart's rhythm, it is possible to generate a coherent heart rhythm simply by breathing slowly and regularly at a 10-second rhythm (5 seconds on the in-breath and 5 seconds on the out-breath)." So why is coherence so important when it comes to breathing? The Institute also states, "input generated by the heart's rhythmic activity is actually one of the main actors that affect our breathing rate and patterns, when the heart's rhythm shifts into coherence as a result of a positive emotional shift, our breathing rhythm automatically synchronizes with the heart, thereby reinforcing and stabilizing the shift to system-wide coherence."[1]

In short, heart coherence is when your heart, mind, and body are in balance and harmony. In this state you are more relaxed and have increased cognitive function, so you are in a better position to learn, complete a task, and make better decisions. Consistently seeking out this synchronization will prove valuable, especially in the early stages of your Intentionality journey, where you are first intuiting how you want to feel and what prolonged physiological changes may be necessary to pave and maintain that path.

Step One: *Inhale for five seconds; exhale for five seconds.*

Find a position where you can sit upright. Close your eyes and begin focusing on your breath, breathing in and out through the nose.

Step Two: *As you continue with the five-count breathing, focus on how to elongate the breath.*

Really focus on the temperature of the breath coming in and out, how your nostrils feel, and on the role they are playing in pulling air in and pushing air out. Notice how identifying with the sensations makes you feel more present in this moment.

Step Three: *Find the connection between the inhale and exhale.*

Feel the air you are inhaling and try to follow its journey back out through your nose. I like to imagine a pair of nostrils on my heart. I imagine them pumping oxygen outward toward my bronchial tree—as if they are having a conversation. I imagine all my parts coming together at my heart, at the center of my being, at exactly that moment to grant me that breath. It feels cyclical—and never-ending.

This is circular breathing, in which each breath flows smoothly into the other. Our inhaling and exhaling are meant to be fluid, to remind us that what we take in, we put back out into the world. Find how this fluid motion of breath helps you reconnect with yourself, how it connects you to others, and how it can further the full-circle sensation of feeling.

Step Four: *Bring your feelings forward.*

While focusing on your heart, slow your breathing down. Repeat five rounds of the same inhaling and exhaling, but slow the pacing down with each series of breaths. Slowing can allow you to feel suspended in the moment, and during this suspension, I want you to bring forward a memory—a time when you really felt nurtured, cared for, or appreciated, or when you were able to nurture, care for, or appreciate something or someone else. This can be a time that you felt nurtured, cared for, or appreciated by yourself, as well. Try to feel how your heart and your breath felt in those moments and bring them forward. Keep breathing, and do your best to bring that experience into the present moment.

Bringing forward a memory to invoke feeling is not the only path to intentional breathing and feeling. You can visualize a color that inspires love, gratitude, and supportive energy, and on the exhale, you can imagine bringing those experiences forward and letting them flow out of you.

In either case, remember to keep an eye on your breath. Notice when you are feeling calm and peaceful. Notice when your breath and your heart feel synchronized, as if they are optimizing your body into a state of rhythm and clarity.

And note that rhythm and clarity are not the only out-comes here.

You have now optimized your system.

You have given shape and texture to what it means to be anchored in the present moment.

KEY TAKEAWAYS

- Breath is our spirit, our life force, and it is a common thread in all spiritual texts.

- Breathing is a function of the autonomic nervous system but differs from other processes because we can also consciously choose to control it—this is what is meant by the term *breathwork*.

- Circuit breakers, our term for conscious breath exercises, create the necessary pause needed to respond rather than react to triggers.

- Breath and heart coherence will get you in the best state to learn, complete tasks, and make decisions.

- You are always just one breath away from Intentionality—practice Heart Coherence Breathing now to reset your whole system.

CHAPTER 2

ONE MIND

Now that we've established the importance of the breath in your Intentionality journey, we're next going to explore how your multilayered mind will factor into this process. Let's begin by looking at the Universal Mind, otherwise referred to as the mind of God, the mind of the absolute—or, in physics, the unified field. The Universal Mind is omnipresent, which means it exists everywhere at all times and encompasses everything that ever was and everything that will be. That includes the subconscious and conscious minds of all of us.

It's omniscient, which means it is all knowing. It's omnificent, which means it is all creative. And perhaps most importantly, it's omnipotent—the all-powerful that lies within each of our individual minds and contains boundless knowledge and wisdom waiting to be activated or manifested. Refer to the diagram on page 10, where we lay out the shape and interconnectivity of what you're working with.

The Universal Mind is represented by the largest circle:

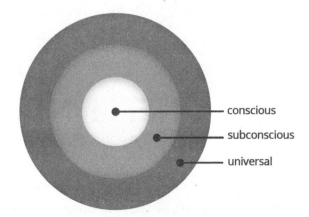

conscious

subconscious

universal

The next circle within it represents your subconscious mind. Your subconscious includes all the mental processes happening below the level of consciousness. I often describe it as the intelligence tapped into from the Universal Mind but now materialized into human form. The subconscious contains all of your autonomic functions and runs everything from how you breathe to how you eat—and notably, it is where your emotions and learned behaviors reside. At its core, the subconscious is focused on making our lives easier.

But it's also subjective. It doesn't have the ability to choose truth or untruth—it's fed the assumptions and the stories we give it.

And last, your subconscious is a survival mechanism. To best understand this, consider that animals exist at the level of the subconscious mind. They feel, but they are not consciously thinking. Instead, they are operating on autopilot, doing whatever they need to do to survive, and do not move past this level. Similarly, without conscious intervention, whatever emotions you, a human being, have at this level are functioning out of survival mode. This means that without consciously overriding your existing coding, you too would stay at this level—creating infinite, suboptimal impressions on both your subconscious mind and the Universal Mind.

Then we have the next circle, which is your conscious mind. Your conscious mind contains mental processes that you are aware of at any given moment. These are your thoughts, sensations, or anything you can directly experience in the present. This is also the location of logical thinking, rational analysis, and deliberate decision-making—and it is all influenced by your environment and your experiences. And it too receives information from your subconscious mind. This is where the choice to consciously override the information from your subconscious mind becomes a critical part of your path to Intentionality and, in particular, your recoding process.

So what does this meeting of the minds actually mean? It means that all too often, we get caught up in our conscious thinking mind and forget that we actually have a subconscious mind, driven by our feelings. And on top of that, we have the Universal Mind, this all-knowing intelligence, available to us at all times. This chapter, and this book as a whole, is about asking and answering some extraordinarily mindful questions like: How can we consciously impress upon our subconscious what our desires are? How can we then allow that to fold into the Universal Mind, to tap into source energy and to embrace the notion that we are all infinite, divine beings?

If you take the diagram and expand the interconnectivity it describes even further—by, for example, adding more layers of subconscious and conscious circles, the ones that exist beyond your own—you can see that we are all connected and that many minds make one. That's when you begin to understand that consciously impressing your desires upon your subconscious can have incremental impacts on other people and on the collective consciousness of us all.

Let's take a closer look at each of these puzzle pieces.

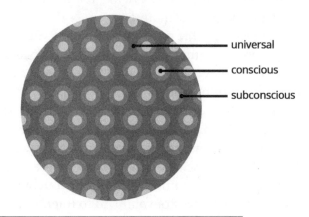

universal

conscious

subconscious

Your Subconscious Mind

In our brains is the paleomammalian cortex—commonly referred to as the limbic system. Simply put, it's the circuitry, wiring, and collection of cerebral structures behind human emotion, memory, instinct, and mood.

A *Nature Reviews Neuroscience* study found in an Early Childhood Education Report noted that when the cortisol levels in a pregnant mother are high, the "developing neural circuitries that make up the limbic system are affected."[1] Additionally, a study in *Brain Research Review* showed that "the fetus responds to the cues it receives and builds its emerging limbic system pathways for a high stress environment."[2] I suppose it's no wonder we have a hard time letting go of the way things have been said or done in the past. We are wired to accommodate these environmental stressors even before we are born.

For years, I've been fascinated by the research and findings of developmental biologist Bruce Lipton. In fact, much of how I've come to understand and evolve my own work with Intentionality has been inspired by the questions Lipton raises about what happens to human beings before they develop consciousness. Recognized for his controversial but enlightening book, *The Biology of Belief*, Lipton argues that our beliefs control our bodies and minds, and as such, our lives. And in an effort to explain how we develop our beliefs and ultimately our way of life, he asks us to turn to the first seven years of human life.

Lipton often points to the saying, "Give me a child until age seven and I will show you the man."[3] According to Lipton, the first seven years of our lives are when we download behaviors observed by our parents, silbings, and the people in our direct community. Lipton points out that "Of the downloaded behaviors acquired before age 7, the vast majority—70 percent or more—are programs of limitation, disempowerment, and self-sabotage."[4]

Our subconscious mind is like a sponge, soaking up information and experiences from a very young age. During our formative years, we are highly impressionable, and our beliefs and perceptions are easily influenced by our environment, family, friends, and society. Negative coding can take root here and play a critical role in shaping the belief loops that define our quality of life.

What I find particularly compelling about Lipton's observations and ultimately his guidance on this matter is that he distinguishes between the functional realities of the subconscious coding we all acquire and the conscious mind that empowers a creative existence. If we know that between the womb and seven years old, we are downloading the habits and beliefs of the people around us, then the burden the conscious mind takes on as early as seven is quite extraordinary.

When my siblings and I were young, we witnessed a volatile marriage. This is not to say that love never existed in our house; it was doled out to us from time to time. But it was elusive and conditional, and any feelings of love were usually eclipsed by negativity. Because of this, for many years, I was driven to seek independence to avoid the pain I associated with love.

Lipton says that the reason it's difficult to live in harmony with subconscious programs formed at a young age and the conscious mind that sets in as we get older is that sooner or later, we pick up on the fact that what we get and what we want are in conflict with each other. I think at seven years old, to some degree, I began learning how I wanted to feel. But the truth is that it wasn't until I was much closer to 37 that I was able to believe I deserved it. In fact, it wasn't until then that I truly understood that wanting to avoid pain is not the same thing as wanting to feel love.

Your subconscious mind is constantly seeking patterns and making associations based on your experiences. So if, for example, you had a negative experience in a particular situation, your subconscious may form coding to avoid similar situations in the future to protect you from potential harm.

Moreover, your subconscious is highly influenced by your emotions. When you experience strong emotions like fear, shame, or guilt, your subconscious takes note and may code you to avoid similar emotional triggers in the future, even if those triggers are not inherently harmful.

This negative subconscious coding can continue to influence your beliefs, thoughts, and behaviors for your entire life. But by becoming aware of your deeply ingrained coding, you can take steps to challenge and replace it with more empowering and positive beliefs, leading to profound personal transformation.

Your Conscious Mind

Now that you understand the power of your subconscious mind and the unequivocal need to consciously interact with it, we need to explore what exactly your conscious mind does for you. To be conscious is to be aware—and the simplest way to explain your conscious mind is to say that in a perfect world, it would be the filter for your coding.

Remember, you have a tremendous amount of coding that happens before the age of seven. In fact, your conscious mind doesn't even develop until that age. This means that your subconscious mind is vulnerable to impressions and to the belief loops of those around you.

So, what is happening when you realize you didn't like the nicknames you were called as a child? Or that you didn't like being labeled as shy, smart, or funny? What happens when you figure out that there are certain ways you don't want to feel again?

Well, with age, you develop a conscious mind, a top layer that allows you to override coding you no longer have an interest in dealing with.

The key to this override is getting your conscious mind—specifically its desires and aspirations—aligned with the coding in your subconscious. Only when these two are aligned can you find inner peace.

Although your conscious mind might be the least powerful of the three minds, it's the most important part. And that's because it gives you choice. Your conscious mind enables you to determine what coding you want to live with. And its most important roles rest in two areas.

First, the conscious mind sends direction to the subconscious for what it wants; this is how it uses its masculine qualities of decision-making and direction. Second, it shields the subconscious from other influences or negative impressions that are in conflict with your desired creation. Once again, it invokes the masculine energy, acting as a gatekeeper and protector.

Your conscious mind effectively becomes your coder. When you acutely tune in to it, you have a heightened state of awareness. You begin to realize that the things that are driving your thoughts, behaviors, and feelings might not actually be true. The conscious mind is your biggest opportunity for self-inquiry, for you to finally be able to ask present-minded questions like, "Is this true? Is this really serving me? What am I contributing to this situation?" So even though the subconscious mind is what determines most of your daily decisions, it is the conscious mind that has the power to identify them, challenge them, and then recode them in real time.

An important and fascinating note about all this, and particularly about the untapped potential the conscious mind may have at scale, is in the conversation around power. People in power typically understand the power of the mind—and how to manipulate it and use it to their advantage. They know that keeping people in survival mode is a means to retaining a strong-hold over them. They understand that fear, blind acceptance, and codependency require ignoring consciousness. Have you ever given away the agency of your conscious mind to others? Have you trusted other people's minds over your own? If you're unsure of your own personal experience, just know that religion, politics, and groupthink give us many noteworthy examples of these power grabs.

Too often we have assumed, because someone is in a position of power, that they are giving us correct information. And in some cases, we have assumed that the information they give us is with our best interest, well-being, and safety at top of mind. Often when we look into humanitarian crises or great human tragedies, we find that the heart of the story is that large swaths of people lost connection with their conscious minds and adopted indifference and inhumanity because of this assumption. But as we move further toward a world that employs artificial intelligence (AI) at scale, it will become critically important for everyone, including you, to power up your conscious mind and question the world around you.

Right now, we are being told that AI can replace jobs in sectors across the globe. And maybe that's true. Maybe it's not. Maybe there will always be jobs that can only be done by humans. What I know for certain is that making people afraid of it works in the favor of systems wanting to control us. Failing to regulate it without explaining its capabilities to the general population is also a problem. And all these actions are being taken by people in power—particularly those who understand the power of the mind.

So whether it's deep-fake news stories, fabricated images, the rise of misinformation, or hive mind conformity, maintaining conscious awareness of your system—and its interaction with the systems of power around you—will prove critical to the collective consciousness and to your own individual quality of life.

The Universal Mind

After learning about the roles belief loops and impressions play within your subconscious mind and the role your conscious mind plays in your daily experiences, let's return to where we started this chapter—with the Universal Mind. Think of it like one source of superintelligence. Everything that exists in nature and has ever existed is connected to the Universal Mind—a force that is all knowing, all feeling, all creating, and that you and everyone around you are manifestations of.

When you connect to the Universal Mind, you will find yourself out of survival mode and engulfed in unconditional love. Max Planck, the father of quantum theory, said, "I regard consciousness as fundamental. I regard matter as a derivative from consciousness. We cannot get behind consciousness. Everything that we talk about, everything that we regard as existing, postulates consciousness."[5]

To me, this means that while you have three minds you are working with, ultimately there is really one mind that connects every being. Some people may refer to this as the creator, God, or the absolute. And because the absolute is omnipresent, this means that it flows through everything. A simpler way of putting this is that there is a singular source of infinite energy available to every single person—a source that is spiritual, not material.

Renowned psychiatrist Dr. David Hawkins talked a lot about this. He said that one of the most important differentiators in quality of life is in whether or not a person believes their source of life is material or spiritual. When they believe it's material, they're stuck in the realm of the intellect. This is, unfortunately, where most of us reside—and this is because we give reason and logic so much overarching power and credibility that we have limited ourselves in areas beyond intellect.

But by accessing the Universal Mind, we can reach the highest energy source and the spiritual realm.

The Brain Connection

A mistake we often make is conflating our mind with our brain.

There is no one place you can point to and say, "There it is. That's my mind." You may have been conditioned to believe that your mind is located only in your head, but it's all over your body. And you know this because you can bring awareness into your hands, for example, through concentration. When you focus your energy there, you can feel your mind in your hands. Your mind is the awareness and the presence. It's everything without separation. It's the thinking, the feeling, the beliefs, and the spiritual form. And most importantly, it's not physically located anywhere.

But your brain is different. You can pinpoint it as a tangibility. That's because your brain itself is a physical tool of your mind—not the other way around. Your brain is the actual material resource responsible for the physical applications in your body. And critically, your brain wave states and the breath you access during these states are what will help you effectively and efficiently move between minds, find greater meaning in your Intentionality journey, and tap into your higher self. Every brain wave state offers unique gifts, perspectives, and opportunities for conscious creation—and as you learn to navigate them, you will gain access to the transformative power of the subconscious mind and the infinite wisdom of the Universal Mind.

Here we'll take a closer look at what's happening within each state, starting from the deep subconscious:

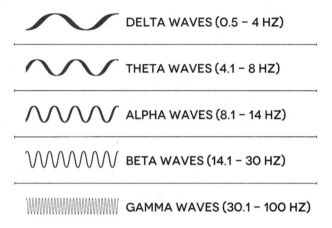

Delta: In delta, the conscious mind is turned off. Here you'll find the slowest band of recordable brain wave frequencies; these are usually associated with deep sleep, the REM cycle, and dreaming—but they're also attainable in a waking state by experienced meditators. Infants have the most access to this state because of the amount of sleep they require. This is a trancelike state where you can access the deepest levels of relaxation and restorative benefits and where you'll have the greatest access to the Universal Mind.

Theta: When you start to wake up or when you're winding down to go to sleep, you are moving into your theta state. For me, it's a beautiful, dreamlike place. I feel like I'm floating on a cloud, straddling the dreaming and waking states. If you've had a good night's sleep, it can feel ethereal, like you're in this precious haze before the chaos of the day. What I love most about theta is that while in it, I don't think about my body or remember my problems—which is to say, I'm feeling a kind of omnipresence and infinite possibility with my state of being. In this moment, the conscious mind is on just enough to send a signal and to keep you aware of your state. This state is where the subconscious is most impressionable and where you can access deep spiritual connection.

Alpha: Once you come through the theta state, you move into alpha. When I'm in alpha, I may have some thoughts, but I don't get attached to them. They come and go. It's a really marvelous place of focus and clarity while remaining calm and Zen. This is also where the balance between the feminine and masculine energies lies. When you are in this place, you can most readily access your intuition. You can tap into the subconscious mind while your conscious mind is also activated. Because alpha is a gateway between the two, it is also the optimal state for observation—this is the goal of meditation. You will notice that in this state you can witness without judgment.

Beta: When you transition from alpha to beta, you will feel fully awake, like that moment a hypnotist snaps his fingers and you come to attention. I've experienced this as a period of being very alert, focused, and engaged. In the beta state, you have access to analytical problem-solving, judgment, logical decision-making, and actively processing the information you receive from the world around you. This is the state that drives your conscious thinking.

Gamma: Gamma is the brain wave with the fastest frequency, and it's the place we're in during extreme concentration. This is a high processing state—what people often refer to as the "flow state," because it's a period in which we are firing on all cylinders. Gamma is the state I'm in when doing extreme adventures—meaning that even when there is high risk involved, I'm not tense, because I've honed into this focused state. By being in what feels like a superconscious state, I'm able to eliminate the stress and fear that would often prevent me from reaching and staying in flow. My belief is that when we're in this state, we're becoming a channel for divine guidance. To activate gamma, tune in to the love frequency, connect to feelings of gratitude, and stay concentrated on the moment—it will bring you to a heightened state of consciousness that leaves you wide open to possibilities.

By now you've fully visualized the meeting of your minds, and you've discovered their interconnectivity and how to access them by regulating your different brain wave states. Now you're ready to use the next circuit breaker and take your next steps inward on the Journey of the Minds, a breath exercise and visualization that will help you traverse the infinite paths to transformation.

Circuit Breaker:
Journey of the Minds

Step One: *Sit or lie down comfortably, eyes closed, and breathe in and out through the nose.*

Begin by closing your eyes. Start paying attention to your breath. Drop out of your head and into your body. Just be here right now, in the present moment, becoming more and more relaxed, more and more grounded. Now imagine a vast ocean with different layers representing the conscious, subconscious, and Universal Minds. You are a skilled diver exploring the depths of your mind.

Step Two: *Take a long, slow deep breath in and hold your air at the top of the inhale.*

Now take a slow, deep breath in. As you're breathing in, I want you to see yourself at the surface of the water, where the waves dance under the sunlight. Here lies the realm of the Conscious Mind. It is the thinking mind with which you interact with the external world, making plans and executing tasks with clarity and precision. In this realm, your brain waves dance in the beta state. It is the state of wakefulness and alertness, where your thoughts are sharp and focused like the peaks of the waves. As you hold your breath, connect to your Conscious Mind, honoring it for all that it does.

Step Three: *Let out an audible exhale through the mouth.*

Now let all your breath out with a big sigh.

Step Four: *Take a long, slow deep breath in and hold your air at the top of the inhale.*

Now take a nice, long, deep breath in again. As you dive deeper, you enter the realm of the subconscious mind, a mysterious and vast expanse where memories, emotions, and beliefs are stored. Here, the waters are calm and ancient wisdom resides, shaping our perceptions and reactions without conscious awareness. Your mind becomes more receptive to insights and creativity, and your brain waves shift to the alpha and theta states.

As you hold your breath, honor the alpha waves that bring relaxation and a sense of calm, like the gentle ebb and flow of the tides. Then honor the theta waves that take you even deeper into the ocean, akin to the gentle, minimal movement of the coral deep beneath the surface. It is in these two states that you can access memories, heal emotional wounds, and connect with your deeper self.

Step Five: *Let out an audible exhale through the mouth.*

Let all your breath out once more with a big sigh.

Step Six: *Take a final elongated deep breath in and hold your air at the top of the inhale.*

On this breath, you are traveling to the bottom of the ocean floor, beyond the depths of the conscious and sub-conscious minds and into the final realm, the Universal Mind. This is the place of inspiration, insight, and universal wisdom where you experience the interconnectedness of all life. Here, your brain waves slow down to the delta state, mimicking the deep, serene depths of the ocean. It is in this state of profound stillness that you can transcend the limitations of the individual self and merge with the Universal Mind. It is a state of oneness where you feel connected to all of existence, like a drop merging into the vastness of the ocean.

Step Seven: *Let out an audible exhale through the mouth.*

On this final exhale, enjoy the peacefulness of the moment. You have gone on a great journey through the minds and honored the importance and unique gifts of the conscious, subconscious, and Universal Minds individually and as a system.

As you read on through this book, you will continue to dive fearlessly into the depths of your mind and discover endless treasures that await you!

KEY TAKEAWAYS

Your Subconscious Mind

- Your subconscious mind is like a sponge, soaking up information and experiences in your environment and is most impressionable from 0 to 7 years of age.

- Your subconscious mind contains all your autonomic functions and is where emotions and learned behaviors reside.

- Try to recall one saying or behavior that you heard or observed repeatedly in your early childhood years that may have influenced your subconscious mind.

Your Conscious Mind

- The conscious mind is your present moment awareness and where logical thinking, rational analysis, and deliberate decision-making take place.

- The two most important roles of the conscious mind are to be the director and the protector.

- Identify some areas in your life where you may have given away the agency of your conscious mind to others.

The Universal Mind

- The Universal Mind is a superintelligence—the all-powerful, all-knowing, all-feeling, infinite source of energy available to all of us.

- When you access the Universal Mind, you can reach the highest energy source and tap into the spiritual realm.

- Reflect on a time when you have felt the all-encompassing power of unconditional love—this was you connecting to the Universal Mind.

The Brain Connection

- The mind and the brain are two different things—one is omnipresent, and one is a physical tool with a precise location in your body.

- There are five main brain wave states you should know of:

    Delta—sleepy/dreaming
    Theta—drowsy/meditative
    Alpha—peaceful/reflective
    Beta—alert/focused
    Gamma—active/flow state

- Have a friend read the Journey of the Minds circuit breaker or record yourself reading it so you can close your eyes and participate in the visualization.

CHAPTER 3

ENERGY CENTERS

We are all made of energy. It is important to understand the energy centers of the body because these are areas that can become blocked, stagnant, or misaligned. These types of energy imbalances can lead to physical illness, mental distress, emotional dysregulation, and spiritual disconnect. After long periods of time a blocked area can even cause you to continuously attract negative circumstances. Many of the modalities you will learn throughout the rest of the book will draw attention to these centers and teach you ways to connect with them in order to keep the flow of energy moving in your body.

You may have heard of these centers referred to as *chakras* (Sanskrit for "wheels"). Chakras are thought of as spinning wheels or vortexes of energy aligned along the spine, each associated with specific physical, emotional, and spiritual attributes. These energy centers function as focal points for the flow of life force or vital energy known most commonly as *chi* or *prana*.

Practices like yoga, traditional Chinese medicine, and various other spiritual and religious traditions generally refer to the seven main chakras. Each has an association with a certain color, location in the body, and either a masculine or feminine energy. Important to note is that the concept of feminine and masculine energy is less about gender or biological sex and more about the qualities inherent in these energies. The chakras are also divided into three lower centers and three upper centers, with the heart chakra serving as the bridge. The three lower chakras are associated with foundational aspects of physical and earthly existence, the heart chakra integrates the lower and upper realms, and the three upper chakras are linked to higher consciousness and spiritual connectedness.

You can activate the chakras in a variety of ways—using tones and sounds, bodywork, breathwork, movement, or simply directing your attention to a specific chakra. Chapter 7 goes into some specific directives and examples of energy interventions to inspire you on your own journey.

The below diagram shows the arrangement of the chakras, followed by a list with their Sanskrit names and a brief description of each energy center. In the list note the clues that point to an imbalance, as this will be helpful in identifying your negative core beliefs in the next chapter.

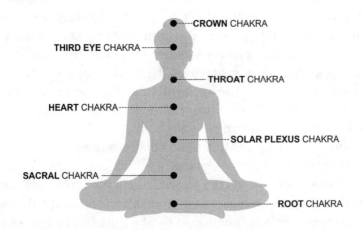

Root (Muladhara)
Location: Base of the spine
Associated with: Survival instincts, safety, stability,
    basic needs
Color: Red
Energetic association: Masculine
Physical manifestations: Legs, feet, bones, adrenal glands
Imbalance: Fear, insecurity, instability

Sacral (Svadhisthana)

Location: Lower abdomen, below the navel

Associated with: Creativity, sexuality, emotional expression, pleasure

Color: Orange

Energetic association: Feminine

Physical manifestations: Reproductive organs, lower back, bladder

Imbalance: Emotional issues, lack of creativity, intimacy issues

Solar Plexus (Manipura)

Location: Upper abdomen, between the navel and sternum

Associated with: Personal power, confidence, self-esteem, willpower

Color: Yellow

Energetic association: Masculine

Physical manifestations: Digestive system, stomach, liver, pancreas

Imbalance: Low self-esteem, lack of confidence, digestive issues

Heart (Anahata)

Location: Center of the chest

Associated with: Love, compassion, connection for mind-body-spirit, relationships

Color: Green

Energetic association: Feminine

Physical manifestations: Heart, lungs, circulatory system

Imbalance: Difficulty in giving or receiving love, hysteria, heartache

Throat (Vishuddha)

Location: Throat

Associated with: Communication, self-expression, truth

Color: Blue

Energetic association: Masculine

Physical manifestations: Throat, neck, thyroid gland

Imbalance: Communication issues, fear of speaking
    truth, thyroid problems

Third Eye (Ajna)

Location: Above and between the eyebrows

Associated with: Intuition, perception, imagination

Color: Purple

Energetic association: Feminine

Physical manifestations: Brain, eyes, pituitary gland

Imbalance: Lack of clarity, difficulty making
    decisions, headaches

Crown (Sahasrara)

Location: Top of the head

Associated with: Spirituality, consciousness,
    higher awareness

Color: White

Energetic association: Masculine

Physical manifestations: Central nervous system,
    pineal gland

Imbalance: Lack of spiritual connection, disconnected
    from higher self

Circuit Breaker:
Chakra Clearing Breath

This breath will allow the energy to rise through all the seven chakras of your body and will leave you focused and full of vitality. You will be drawing your attention to each energy center and activating it by directing your breath to its location, illuminating it with its specific color and coding a positive belief into your subconscious with a short affirmative statement. You will be doing box breathing, which consists of a four-count inhale, a four-count hold, a four-count exhale, and a four-count hold.

Step One: *Sit or lie down comfortably, eyes closed and tongue resting gently on the roof of your mouth.*

As you begin to breathe in the four-count pattern, keep your focus on the breath but not be overly consumed with it. You will be maintaining a dual focus on the body and the breath, dropping into a relaxed and grounded state.

Step Two: *Inhale for four counts and then hold for four counts.*

As you breathe in, draw your attention to the root chakra at the base of your spine. On the hold, flood the area with the color red.

Step Three: *Exhale for four counts and then hold for four counts.*

As you release your breath, say silently to yourself, "I am safe." Revel in this feeling during the four-count hold.

Step Four: *Inhale for four counts and then hold for four counts.*

As you breathe in, draw your attention to the sacral chakra in the lower abdomen below the navel. On the hold, flood the area with the color orange.

Step Five: *Exhale for four counts and then hold for four counts.*

As you release your breath, say silently to yourself, "I am nurtured and cared for." Revel in this feeling during the four-count hold.

Step Six: *Inhale for four counts and then hold for four counts.*

As you breathe in, draw your attention to the solar plexus chakra in the upper abdomen between the navel and the sternum. On the hold, flood the area with the color yellow.

Step Seven: *Exhale for four counts and then hold for four counts.*

As you release your breath, say silently to yourself, "I am worthy." Revel in this feeling during the four-count hold.

Step Eight: *Inhale for four counts and then hold for four counts.*

As you breathe in, draw your attention to the heart chakra in the center of the chest. On the hold, flood the area with the color green.

Step Nine: *Exhale for four counts and then hold for four counts.*

As you release your breath, say silently to yourself, "I am loved." Revel in this feeling during the four-count hold.

Step Ten: *Inhale for four counts and then hold for four counts.*

As you breathe in, draw your attention to the throat chakra in the throat and neck. On the hold, flood the area with the color blue.

Step Eleven: *Exhale for four counts and then hold for four counts.*

As you release your breath, say silently to yourself, "I am connected to my truth." Revel in this feeling during the four-count hold.

Step Twelve: *Inhale for four counts and then hold for four counts.*

As you breathe in, draw your attention to the third-eye chakra above and between the eyebrows. On the hold, flood the area with the color purple.

Step Thirteen: *Exhale for four counts and then hold for four counts.*

As you release your breath, say silently to yourself, "I am aware." Revel in this feeling during the four-count hold.

Step Fourteen: *Inhale for four counts and then hold for four counts.*

As you breathe in, draw your attention to the crown chakra at the top of your head. On the hold, flood the area with the color white.

Step Fifteen: *Exhale for four counts and then hold for four counts.*

As you release your breath, say silently to yourself, "I am whole." Revel in this feeling during the four-count hold.

Step Sixteen: *Take one last final inhale and one last big exhale.*

Using your longest, slowest breath, inhale—traveling up through all the chakras, feeling the open flow of energy starting at the base of the spine and up to the crown. There is no need to count now; just focus on the breath raising your vibration through each energy center. Then exhale fully, from the top of the crown down to the base of the spine, releasing completely.

You can now rest and breathe normally, letting the breath adjust to its own natural rhythm. Give yourself a few moments in meditation and notice if any specific part of the body is calling out to you. You can revisit that chakra and breathe into it as long as you intuitively feel it needs. Trust that you know what you are doing, because no one knows your body as well as you do.

KEY TAKEAWAYS

- Chakras are energy centers in the body, each with its own physical, emotional, and spiritual attributes.

- When your energy centers become blocked, this can result in mental distress, physical illness, emotional dysregulation, and spiritual disconnect.

- There are seven main chakras starting from the base of the spine to the top of the head: root, sacral, solar plexus, heart, throat, third eye, and crown.

- Close your eyes and do a body scan—notice where you feel a sensation of any type. It may be tingling, numbness, warmth or coolness—anything at all that grabs your attention. Identify which chakra location this is aligned to and see if the imbalance associated with that energy center brings forward something that rings true for you.

Part II

YOUR
CODING

The important thing is not to stop questioning.
Curiosity has its own reason for existing.

— **ALBERT EINSTEIN**

CHAPTER 4

BELIEF LOOPS

In an article for the American Vaudeville Museum, Victoria Esposito wrote about the history of plate-spinning: "In China, plate spinning was seen in acrobatic groups where they would all work together to simultaneously twirl dishes in a choreographed routine." She went on to note this important evolution: "When plate spinning migrated to western culture, the plate spinner worked alone."[1] I'm fascinated by the fact that in one culture, this skill was considered a team effort, and when it showed up here, we chose to turn it into an individual act. Erich Brenn made a name for himself wowing television audiences on *The Ed Sullivan Show* in the 1950s and '60s.

When you take a second look at something long viewed as a funny vaudeville amusement, you realize that the whole allure of westernized plate spinning is that it's one person versus multiple poles and plates. The thrill is in whether or not the individual, in this case Erich Brenn, will be able to keep everything balanced and in motion. The thrill is in whether or not the other plates will drop.

For as cheeky as my analogy may be, when we think about society's knowing and unknowing efforts to keep what I've identified as negative belief loops spinning, this is what it can often feel like. Being outnumbered, outrun, or manipulated by the systems that are spun for us—and that we eventually keep spinning ourselves—can feel exhausting.

This chapter will explore the anatomy of belief loops, share with you my experiences of my own core belief loops, and embolden you to create positive belief loops of your own.

Designed to inspire and guide you through how to best reclaim your agency and harness the intelligence of your subconscious mind, this deeper exploration of belief-loop formation and challenges will introduce you to your own coding and further prepare you for the recoding process.

Here's the thing—beliefs are just beliefs. They are stories we tell ourselves. And while everyone is entitled to their own beliefs, it is helpful to ask yourself these questions: Are your beliefs serving you? How do you differentiate whether they are serving or sabotaging you? What are the determinants that make up your beliefs? Figuring this out is all part of the magic of regaining control of your system.

The Anatomy of a Belief Loop

During a speaking engagement in 2008, Dr. David Hawkins explained to an audience his theory that in order to survive, the human mind must oscillate in a fairly frustrating state.

He talked about the mind as though it were a machine, a system—something he said that "keeps itself busy, dreaming up problems for the future, and inventing regrets over the past,"[2] constantly going forward and backward and leaving a person in a perpetual state of nonreality. This description resonated with me immediately.

I could envision and feel those times when I had ping-ponged back and forth between regrets of the past and anxieties of the future. It was a sensation that mimicked an arcade pinball—one that felt really heavy but was also swift and merciless in how it darted up, down, and around the tunnels and pockets of my machine. And while listening to Hawkins's description, I felt an intense physical and emotional relief in knowing that someone out there seemed intimately familiar with the struggles I and so many others were having. It was frightening how easily I could go from overthinking something to running away from it entirely. There was no in-between—only the frenetic, immediate necessity to avoid any feelings of confusion, doubt, or stress.

Susan Hawkins, David's wife, who was also on stage with him during this talk, wanted David to explain that if this was the case, if we were all machines who were in some ways perpetually in motion, locked into our penchant for nostalgia or fueling our engine with anxiety, then what could be done? She made a circular motion, spinning with her finger—implying that we all spin, that we are all caught in these loops, and that we all struggle to break our bad habits. I knew she was right, and I wondered: If that really was the case, how could we truly ever let go and just live?

Watching this talk inspired me to spend more time visualizing all the parts that played a role not just in how people function, but particularly in how we feel. Human beings contextualize history in timelines. When we look at a story, we are coded to want a sensible presentation—a horizontal line that, in Western culture, trains our eye from left to right, in a linear fashion, walking us through the ins and outs of where we came from, how we got here, and where we're going. That left-to-right, linear mindset we all have is a subconscious element of order. If we lose the line, we not only lose order, but we also lose control. This is where the catch comes in.

Ultimately life is circular. Circular implies dimension, meaning, symmetry, and closure. Humans love a happy ending. We love something or someone who comes full circle. So why, then, is the symbol we find so much positive meaning in also the image that comes to mind when we talk about our bad habits, our destructive patterns, or our spiraling and spinning out of control?

The circle is also at the heart of how we have gamified our existence. We close the rings on a health app to indicate we've gotten our steps and completed our physical goals for the day. On *Wheel of Fortune*, a game show that has captivated audiences for nearly

50 years with the simple concept that when a wheel—widely known as one of humanity's earliest inventions and thematically understood as the symbol of progress—stops, humans are suddenly at a crossroads. And what do they do then? They spin it again. The show's combination of a word clue with the act of spinning the wheel leaves just enough room for people to debate over whether it's a game of luck or personal agency—or both.

Time and again, examples in history have not only subtly and overtly shaped our complicated relationship with circles and our relation to or rejection of linear thinking, but they have also validated another equally important point. While life may be circular, not every circle is a wheel of progress or fortune. For every positive belief loop, we are likely to find a negative one in need of dismantling. We are engaged in complicated relationships with ourselves and our systems. This is a lifelong balancing act between resigning ourselves to the dramatic, negative forces inside of us and harnessing the possibilities that come with positive, intentional living.

Belief Loop

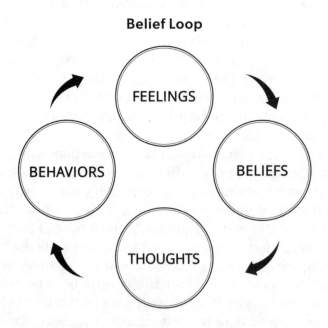

So, what are belief loops, and why do they matter? A belief loop is a circular rotation of beliefs, thoughts, behaviors, and feelings rooted firmly in your system. Because its initial form resides in your subconscious, its negative capabilities require a significant, conscious effort to recode so you can reformulate a healthier, sustainable path forward. In short, belief loops include both the behavioral patterns we succumb to as a result of our beliefs and the biological impact those behavioral patterns then have on our bodies.

It's important to distinguish between the following two variations:

A negative belief loop is the result of a hardwiring and a lifetime of codified beliefs, thoughts, behaviors, and feelings that undermine our potential—it's the product of our subconscious mind essentially going haywire.

A positive belief loop is the result of consciously recoding your system, of your conscious mind overriding codified beliefs, thoughts, behaviors, and feelings, in an effort to return you to your natural rhythm and empower you to live a more intentional way of life.

The Ego

Now is an important time to talk about the ego, because it's the driver behind all negative belief loops. A psychological construct representing an individual's sense of self, the ego is an overidentification with your thoughts, feelings, and your perception of your own existence. The ego itself isn't a problem—but when we attach our *identity* to the ego, we form a false sense of self.

From a scientific perspective, the ego is a crucial aspect of human cognition. It's the contextual lens that you view your life through and what you use to interact with your external environment.

In many spiritual traditions, the ego is considered a temporary and often distorted perception of one's true nature and of the interconnection with the Universal Mind or higher consciousness. This is because the ego is the opposite of collective consciousness, defining itself by its separation of "I" from "others."

Any complaining, blaming, defending, resisting, criticizing, catastrophizing, or defending comes from an egoic place. This doesn't mean that you need to like every situation you are in or that you will always feel positive emotions. One way to tell if a feeling is from the ego is to examine if it is stimulated by a thought in your head, where you are creating a story around it and perhaps making assumptions and taking things personally.

Once you get into a present state, you can observe a negative feeling and let it flow through. This enables you to accept your current experience and take the available actions to change it without adding any extra negative feelings or drama to the situation. In fact, it is impossible for the ego to exist in the present moment. When you are in a present state, you will find that you can remain peaceful in a situation that would normally hijack your emotions and heighten your physiological responses.

The ego is very cunning, so we can't assume that all positive emotions are good for us either. Rather, if they come from a place of presence, then they are good for us. If they come from a place attached to an external factor, then they are ego based. For example, if we get excited and confident about a potential windfall from an investment, we are attaching our happiness to an outcome. Our fantasy can turn into fear once our minds' made-up view of a future situation is dependent on it.

In its most potent form, the ego's tentacles grab hold of you through self-importance or self-identification. Examples of this include when you believe that you are your thoughts or feelings, or even that you are the physical form that makes up your system. None of that is true—but the ego understands the human penchant for identity and importance, and it feeds your mind and body accordingly.

But more than anything else, the ego operates on one negative core belief—"I am not enough." Other versions of this are "I am not worthy," "I am not lovable," and "I am not seen." Each of these negative beliefs is often met with an intense need to be "right"— as if that will somehow make you enough, worthy, loved, or seen in the eyes of others. In fact, nothing strengthens the ego more than that notion of being "right." But to be "right," you need others to be "wrong." This is how the ego stakes its claim within, how it remains driven by fear and a desire to overpower others, and how it goes to great lengths to hold its ground, especially when in conflict (when it feels most threatened). Self-justification, defensiveness, and blaming others all inevitably follow.

The ego likes the known because it exists in the known. It doesn't care whether you are thriving or surviving. This is why we meet so much resistance whenever we attempt to make a change. It's not that change is hard, it's that the ego is trying to justify its existence and will trick you into staying the same.

So much of recoding is about learning to override these distorted perceptions, and that's because recoding is about returning you to your truest nature. And ego is, of course, not who you are in your truest nature. Who you are in your truest nature is someone who rebuffs these attempts by the ego to own you with absolutes. Who you are in your truest nature is someone with self-awareness, not self-importance.

Once you understand the role of coding in the development of your ego, it will open the door to a heightened sense of self-awareness. You can then make the conscious effort to challenge and expand your belief systems and pave a new way, one that serves you and what you desire, by recoding your subconscious.

A good place to start is with a breath that will help you dissolve egocentric tendencies that have a way of staking claim in your system and never leaving. That is, unless you find outlets like this circuit breather: the Ego Dissolution Breath. An exercise created to help you detach from the urge to self-identify, this breath also clears any reliance you might have on self-importance and inspires you to seek out collective consciousness and a higher sense of self.

Circuit Breaker:
Ego Dissolution Breath

The Ego Dissolution Breath is very energizing. It will open your lungs, give you lots of clarity, and help dissolve the hold your ego may have on you at any given moment. It can be really beneficial to do while seated across from another person so that you mirror each other, or you can do it in front of an actual mirror. The type of breathing here is called *fire-breathing*, and it is very active on the exhale and passive on the inhale. You'll breathe forcefully out of the nose at a rapid pace, with the mouth gently closed. Without pausing, force the air out of your nose as your abdomen contracts, focusing solely on the exhale: the inhale will happen naturally. It can be helpful to practice a few rounds of this breath with your hand on your belly to feel the abdomen contracting.

You will be doing 50 rounds of this breath. Adjust to your own rhythm, but make sure you do the exhales in quick succession of one another.

Step One: *Sit in a cross-legged position with your back straight and eyes open.*

As you prepare for this breath, gather your fingers into a fist and leave your thumbs sticking out in the thumbs-up position.

Step Two: *Raise your arms overhead and take an inhale through your nose.*

Your arms should be in a *V* shape with your thumbs pointing up. Be careful not to lift your shoulders.

Step Three: *Begin the breath of fire: sharp exhales out the nose and passive inhales.*

Your exhales should be powerful and loud, your inhales barely noticeable. Do 50 exhales out the nose and take a brief pause on the final exhale.

Step Four: *Take a big inhale in and draw your thumbs together.*

As you inhale, draw your thumbs together above your head until they touch, and direct your gaze to your third eye. Your eyes will be open and crossed as they look up and inward.

Step Five: *Hold your breath, thumbs, and gaze where they are for 30 seconds.*

Keep your thumb tips touching and feel the energy of your body activating while you focus on your third eye.

Step Six: *As you release the breath, draw the thumbs down and place a smile on your face.*

Slowly draw your arms down in front of you as you exhale, elbows out to the side. You will be giving a double thumbs-up sign at this point while smiling brightly. This is really fun when you're staring at a partner, and a great self-love practice when staring at yourself.

Your old coding has no chance of hijacking you if you've done this breath correctly because you will have interrupted its control of your mind and given your body a good clearing.

My Core Belief Loops

For many years, my core negative belief loop was that I would be abandoned. Over the years I've explored the ways in which my early childhood played a role in the formation of this loop and others. From what I've gathered, a traumatic incident with my parents on my 10th birthday led to the development of my subconscious fear of abandonment. As I got older, I carried with me the fear and assumption that anyone I loved would eventually leave me.

Every year on my birthday, I would run into my parents' room at 6:02 in the morning. That was the time of my birth. And even if all the other days of the year in the house were rife with tension and pain, my parents managed to keep it together and make sure that day was full of joy, family, and fun. However, on the morning of my 10th birthday, the tone was very different.

Often my father would leave me in cars while he was at musical gigs, would be late to pick me up, and would keep me at a distant second to the sunsetting of his career as an aging rock star. He loved planning an annual music festival very much in the vein of Woodstock, and he would have his friends and colleagues come perform on our rural property to replicate the musical traditions the elder hippies had so carefully curated over the years. There was absolutely no reason for this festival to take place on my birthday. Regardless, that's what my dad felt was best for this particular year.

I woke up and walked down the hall to my parents' room, still hopeful for the day ahead despite my negative feelings about the festival. But when I reached the doorway, everything felt off. There was a cloud of doom and anger surrounding my father as he looked out the window at the pouring rain. The field was filled with mud, and my father was filled with angst. Instead of greeting me, he said, "Ruined! It's ruined! We're doomed!" My mother sat silently in the bed.

Now, what he said and what I interpreted it to mean were very different things. He was talking about his event being rained out.

What I heard were the ramblings of a father who, yet again, had discarded me for another grasp at stage glory. What I saw was a father who didn't wish me a happy birthday. And when I asked, "Are we going to celebrate my birthday?" he turned around to face me and said, "Fuck off, Finn."

In the grand scheme of things, is a father's outburst the end of the world? Of course not. But in a long line of disappointing behaviors from my father, this was the one that did me in. This was the one there was no coming back from. Not only had he already planned a day where we weren't going to be together on my birthday; he hadn't even considered that it was part of a long pattern of him putting me second. I didn't know at the time that this would be such a a pivotal moment in my life: from there on out, my subconscious mind created a narrative that I would always be abandoned.

Negative Belief Loop

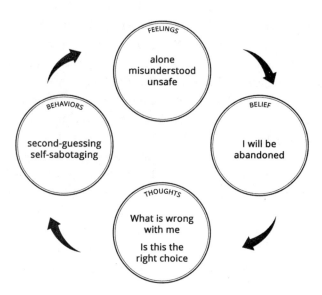

And I kept on telling this story well into my marriage. In fact, I extrapolated further, and my thoughts around my marriage then became: *Is this the right relationship? Can I do better?*

With my behavior, I was always second guessing everything. I was using self-protective language like "We're not obligated to be married forever," both as internal discourse and in a softened-down way to my partner. And I created ways out, like the idea of renewing our commitment every five years. My intent was to be in an extraordinary relationship and ritually celebrate our love, but subconsciously I had created a protection mechanism that perpetuated within me a state of anticipatory grief.

Anticipatory grief is a term describing what we feel about the impending loss of a loved one—someone who may be facing a terminal illness, for example. Looking at the days and months to come, we may try to preemptively lessen the pain we fear we'll have when they pass. But a state of anticipatory grief is an attempt to control our feelings and, in many instances, avoid them altogether. Unfortunately, this protective mechanism ends up hindering our ability to feel present with our loved ones and enjoy our current relationships.

Looking back I can see I was grieving my relationship before it was even gone. And despite my best-laid plans, that behavior played a pivotal role in why it ended in the first place.

This, of course, begs the question: "Was the reality that she abandoned me, or did I manifest the abandonment with my core negative belief loop?" Sarah may have had some awareness of the fears I faced as a result of my childhood, but ultimately the power over recoding that way of life rested with me. If I had had the understanding that I was capable of recoding, and as such, capable of creating my reality, then wouldn't the responsibility for getting clear on the negative loops that I brought to the relationship fall on me?

Once you come to the realization that you are the master of your mind and the architect of your reality, you have the responsibility to recode yourself and the opportunity to build the life you've been searching for.

Ultimately I felt alone, unsafe, and misunderstood for much of my life, and this was the negative belief loop driving my system. At 10 years old, I don't think my conscious mind was developed enough to even comprehend that what had happened with my parents wasn't about me. I couldn't come to terms with the feeling that I wasn't important to them, so I programmed myself to prevent feeling that way again.

In my case, because I couldn't rely on my parents, my negative belief loop around abandonment initially prompted me to seek independence. I became the youngest army officer in Australia at the time, learned how to make money at a young age, established myself as an entrepreneur, and had a lot of recognition and material wealth. The only problem was that this way of life was all born out of what I considered a necessary step in survival—avoiding relationships that could possibly compromise the strength of my resolve. I was so hell-bent on avoiding pain instead of learning to feel it, process it, and learn from it, that in the end, I abandoned myself in the process.

But there is good news! For every negative belief loop running within us, it is possible to create a positive belief loop to override it. You just need to draw awareness to it and be ready to admit that you have a program that's not working for you. Then you need to get curious about becoming a recoder and create a program that works in your favor.

Here's a set of simple questions to help you consciously create your own positive belief loops:

- What are my desired feelings?
- What behaviors would lead to those feelings?
- What thoughts would I need to have to drive those behaviors?
- What positive belief brings this full circle?

Positive Belief Loop

In my case, I desired to feel seen, connected, and safe. I knew that to achieve those feelings, I would have to go inward. I would have to connect to the feelings I was trying to avoid and start committing fully to things—no more half-assing.

I also knew it meant that I would need to shift my perspective around abandonment. I would need to think about the fact that I had nothing to fear, and that ultimately I was in charge of my happiness.

And to complete the cycle of positive belief loop creation, I needed to replace the core belief "I will be abandoned" with "I am accepted."

Now that you have the fundamentals of belief loop origins and overrides under your belt, use these four questions—as well as some simple tips I will lay out next to further explore the transformational possibilities that can come with positive belief loop creation.

Your Belief Loops

Something I often say to people is, "I don't care what you believe. What I care about is that your beliefs are serving you."

To me that is the litmus test for the quality of your life.

To figure out if your beliefs are serving you, you need to first know what to look for. Feelings are your cues. They will alert you to whether your subconscious is working for you or against you. If you're having many negative feelings, or what I refer to as low-vibrational frequencies—fear, separation, anxiety—then you are experiencing a subconscious program that is not working in your favor.

Then you'll need to ask yourself, *What behaviors of mine are driving these feelings?* Because, yes, other people's behaviors factor into how we feel, but ultimately when it comes to Intentionality, we acknowledge that even our reactionary behaviors are still *ours*. There must be ownership there. Because when you take ownership, you will be able to find a causal relationship between your beliefs and your behaviors. You will be able to dig deeper to find the core belief loops that are driving your system and further assess the role you have in recoding it.

When it comes to belief loop origins and overrides, ownership means acknowledging the uncomfortable reality that human beings confuse beliefs with truths. How does this happen? An event occurs that evokes a strong-enough emotion felt within the subconscious. The subconscious registers this as truth and then kicks into autopilot with thoughts and behaviors— which reaffirm the feeling of the false truth and turn it into a deeply embedded belief.

To stop that cycle, start by understanding that an important part of your Intentionality journey will mean questioning your "truths" all the time. One of the most essential steps on your path to Intentionality will be to question the world around you with sincere curiosity and a desire for personal transformation. The act of questioning someone or something can be perceived as inherently negative, but in its purest form, it can be truly enlightening.

Begin with some questions about your early life: Do you know any information or details about your birth? How long was your mother in delivery? Were there complications? How do you define *home*? What cultural beliefs did you grow up with? How did religion (or lack thereof) shape your beliefs? How did your teachers, peers, and education mold your perspectives? What were some of the common sayings that your family taught you? What fears did your family install in you? What goals or dreams did they wish for you to aspire to?

Then try asking probing questions that ensure you don't become hostage to your negative thoughts: Is this thought true? If I act on this thought, will it lead to my desired feelings? Is there another thought from a different perspective that could be equally true? What behaviors would lead me to my desired feelings?

Additionally, try becoming more observant. Seek out your blind spots. Examine how your system's mechanisms are influenced by the world around you. Activate your desire to change, and chart a new path.

Here are some positive beliefs that are a good starting point for your Intentionality journey:

- I am a part of a friendly universe
- I have access to an infinite source of energy providing me with unconditional love
- I am confident, capable, and worthy
- My fulfillment comes from my inner world

After you've asked some questions and adopted some of these positive beliefs to inspire you, try this powerful circuit breaker: Alternate Nostril Breathing. This type of breathing will help you break old patterns, discover your outdated coding, and start to build anew.

Belief loop creation will be enhanced with a number of resources in this book that underscore the circular connection within our system. These include breathwork (circuit breakers), repetition, energy interventions, and the scientific manifestation process. But because we are still in the early stages of your

Intentionality journey, I feel compelled to reiterate the importance of breath in connection with belief loops.

Whenever I'm ruminating over a particular problem or event that has occurred, it's a sign that I'm stuck in a loop. In these moments, I always go back to breath—because breath has proved, time and again, to be the most seamless path for coming into the present moment, to the place where healing and wholeness occurs.

It's not an overstatement to say that positive belief loop creation must begin with breath. It's the one thing that consistently keeps us in the present, never allowing us to stray too far into the past or future, and it pulls us toward the next step on our path. In fact, after decades of struggling with my core negative belief loop, and with the effective creation of an overriding positive belief loop, I learned that a big part of what was holding me back was that I wasn't spending enough of my energy in breathwork. It is the single most effective tool that has enabled me to explore the connections between my mind, body, and energy centers. It's also what empowered me to come full circle and, at long last, to pull myself out of my unprocessed trauma and abandon my interpretations of the past.

This next exercise is designed to help you do just that.

Circuit Breaker:
Alternate Nostril Breathing

The Sanskrit name for alternate-nostril breathing is *nadī shodhana*. *Nadī* is the word for "channel" and *shodhana* means "cleaning." With the two terms combined, you can understand why this is also sometimes called the "channel-cleaning breath." If negative belief loops are the product of excess negative energy building up in your system, you need to first clear the old energy to create any new positive belief loop. Once you've done so, you can then fill yourself with new, clean energy.

When we engage in Alternate Nostril Breathing, we activate both hemispheres of the brain and synchronize their activity. This harmonization of brain function creates a state of mental coherence and balance. As we focus on the breath and move between nostrils, we become more present and aware of our thoughts and feelings.

With this circuit breaker, prepare to bring attention to the breath and the flow of energy in your body. This practice will allow you to calm your mind, release tension, and create a more receptive state of being.

Step One: *Find a comfortable seat, close your eyes, and turn your focus inward.*

Take a moment to focus on your breath, inhaling and exhaling through your nose. Bring your right hand up to your face and place your index and middle fingers between your eyebrows. Rest your right thumb gently on top of the right nostril and your ring finger gently on top of the left nostril.

Step Two: *Inhale for four counts.*

Use your right thumb to close your right nostril, and inhale deeply through your left nostril for a count of four.

Step Three: *Hold your breath for two counts.*

Hold your breath at the top with both nostrils closed for a count of two.

Step Four: *Exhale for six counts.*

Then use your ring finger to close your left nostril and release your right as you exhale for a count of six.

Step Five: *Hold your breath for two counts.*

Hold your breath at the bottom for a count of two.

Step Six: *Repeat on the opposite side.*

Keeping your left nostril closed, inhale deeply through your right nostril for a count of four. Hold your breath with both nostrils closed for a count of two. Then close your right nostril and release your left as you exhale for a count of six. Hold your breath at the bottom for a count of two.

Step Seven: *Repeat Steps Two through Six twice more.*

When complete, you will have done this breathing pattern six times, three on each side.

Step Eight: *Release and observe.*

When you're finished, release your hand from your face and take a moment to observe how you feel.

KEY TAKEAWAYS

Anatomy of a Belief Loop

- A belief loop is a circular rotation of beliefs, thoughts, behaviors, and feelings rooted firmly in your system that can be either negative or positive.

- A belief loop's initial form resides in your subconscious, so its negative capabilities require a significant, conscious effort to recode.

- Think of a long-held belief you have had that would be very difficult to challenge—these kinds of beliefs often have roots in political, religious, or cultural teachings. List the ways that this black-and-white thinking may have served you in the past but is sabotaging you now.

The Ego

- The ego is a psychological construct representing your sense of self; it is the contextual lens that you view your life through and what you use to interact with your external environment.

- The ego itself isn't a problem—it is when we attach our identity to the ego that we form a false sense of self and separate ourselves as "I" from "others."

- Try challenging your ego for a day by using the phrase "Is that so?" as your default response in conversations. Notice how often your ego wants to interject with an opinion and how the people around you respond.

My Core Belief Loop

- Anticipatory grief is a term describing what we feel about the impending loss of a loved one and we often use it as a protective mechanism to control our feelings.

- As the master of your mind and the architect of your reality, you have the responsibility to recode yourself and the opportunity to build the life you've been searching for.

- Identify a negative core belief you hold in your system. Reflect on memories that have reinforced this belief over your lifetime, going as far back as you can remember.

Your Belief Loops

- Feelings are your cues and alert you to whether your subconscious is working for you or against you.

- One of the most essential steps on your path to Intentionality will be to question the world around you with sincere curiosity and a desire for personal transformation.

- Take a stab at your first belief loop creation. What are some of your desired feelings? What behaviors would lead to those feelings? What thoughts would you need to have to drive those behaviors? What positive belief would be at the core of those thoughts? Helpful hint: some of the most common core positive beliefs are "I am enough," "I am worthy," "I am loved," and "I am seen."

CHAPTER 5

IMPRESSIONS

We are impressionable beings. It's hard not to be when so much of our days are tied to external stimulation and influence. From social media to the news to our families and more, the storytelling and personal experiences we are exposed to are inextricably tied to how we ingest and interpret information and how we choose to indict or align ourselves with the beliefs and behaviors of others.

Identifying the impressions that may be lingering in your system can offer some of the most valuable insights into why you feel the way you do about everything from relationships and work to the broader challenges unfolding in the world around you. And once you take a closer look at how they've taken root in your subconscious, you can begin to actively weed out and re-code the unwanted impressions for a more intentional way of life.

Family

For years, I lived my life answering the question, "What do I want?"

It seems harmless enough, but in retrospect, "What do I want?" is the product of social conditioning that goes further back than any one of us are consciously aware of. In the case of the Kelly household, it was always a hot topic. As the son of an aspiring musician and respected doctor, status and prestige were heavily valued. In fact, when I was little, my aunt gave me an activity book that had at the top of the first page the phrase:

This book belongs to:

With it was a black-and-white drawing of a nameplate necklace that I was supposed to fill in. The rest of the book had a series of bizarre, if not alarming, prompts where I was directed to fill in the blanks:

What I wish I'd been called _____.

What my father wanted to call me if I'd been a girl_____.

What my mother wanted to call me if I'd been a girl____.

Unprintable names I get called _____.

Page after page, there were more questions about what I had versus what I wanted—and soon enough, there it was:

What do you want to be when you grow up?

My mother wanted me to be a doctor, like her. But that wasn't something I was interested in—especially because at times, I felt like I only received the love I wanted from her when I was sick or having some kind of medical problem. My mother was a physician first, which is to say that back then, I felt like she took care of me less as her son and more as her patient.

My father was a musician and took more interest in me when I was willing to pick up an instrument. I remember him complaining frequently about money, and yet there was always enough to buy the newest, top-of-the-line instruments. When I showed even the slightest interest in playing one, that's when he was suddenly father of the year, showering me with attention.

Needless to say, my parents' conditional love wasn't the most inspiring or convincing argument for me to take up their professions. But I was inspired by what was missing in our house. At the time my aunt gave me the aforementioned book, I'd written that I wanted to be a dad. I wrote this because even at that age, I knew I wanted to be a dad, and I also knew in my bones that I didn't want to be like my father. I would be better.

When I recently found this childhood book in a box in storage, I realized that "What do you want to be when you grow up?" is a terrible question to ask a child. It's completely outcome driven. In my case, it felt like my only options were to offend one of my parents or evade the question altogether. And because my family had placed such an intense priority on success, it conditioned me to think that my identity was only ever going to be wrapped up in what I did for a living or what I contributed to society.

In fairness, at face value, the questions "What do you want?" or "What do you want to be?" make sense. Asking someone what they want isn't intrinsically a fruitless endeavor or rooted in some kind of malice. Outcomes aren't inherently problematic. The problem is that the people around you have likely learned to ask these questions through an external and materialistic lens. And on top of that, they're putting the cart before the horse.

When it came to my family, not once did anyone ever ask, "How do you want to feel?" And if you think about it, you'll understand that this is the question that should come first. Why? Because despite good intentions, when family members who "mean well" ask about your life's path, they are doing so in the context of their own social conditioning. They have likely learned to want a car, a job, a partner, a house, a baby, and a retirement plan—in that order. And that's because in any capitalist society, these answers have historically been tethered to materialism. But had your family asked first the question of how you want to feel, the answers would be driven by an internal exploration of your mind, of what would evoke a greater sense of wholeness and inner peace. And once you were able to answer that, you could better elucidate a job or circumstance that might support your overall well-being.

Family members, by definition, always have a lasting impression on your life story. These are the people who, for better or worse, have played a role in molding you from the earliest version of yourself to who you are today. And this is especially true if you are not estranged or if you've grown up (and/or remained) in close proximity to your loved ones. Because not only are you genetically tied to these people, you're environmentally exposed to them on a frequent basis. And whether you embraced or rejected the viewpoints and lessons espoused in your household, growing up in the same space undoubtedly had an impact on your beliefs and behaviors. It's up to you to break the mold and carve your own way forward. Maybe you can take your first cues from my experience and start by changing the conversation.

Language

Family isn't the only mold that, at times, needs to be broken. Language casts a certain spell on us. We are deeply influenced by sayings and clichés that we grew up hearing, and so often, rather than question these dated expressions, we equate their frequency of use with efficacy and meaning.

Much like how I have drawn the connection between the symbolism of circles and why they might be deeply rooted in our world view, it's not difficult to further connect the dots on the words that have imprinted on us—and in particular the ill-advised mantras that perpetuate a culture of illusion. These codified clichés and sayings that have been passed down to us are slogans devoid of feeling and written to reinforce cycles of absolutism.

Let's dive into a few of the most pervasive.

No pain, no gain.

Some version of this phrase has plagued humanity since at least Sophocles, who wrote in *Electra* that nothing truly succeeds without pain. Robert Herrick's brief poem titled "No Paines, No Gaines," published in 1648, had in it only two lines:

If little labour, little are our gains;
Man's fortunes are according to his paines.[1]

And in the late 20th century, Jane Fonda made the phrase "no pain, no gain" popular with her successful series of exercise videos, and we saw this mantra permeate the fitness world.

Interestingly, Jeffrey Perlman, the chief marketing officer for one of the most profitable fitness movements in the world, Zumba, realized that this might not be a lasting sentiment. In a 2012 interview with *AdAge*, Perlman recalled seeing a billboard with two dancers in the David LaChapelle film *Rize*.[2]

He said, "I immediately called my brother [Alberto Perlman, the CEO of Zumba] and said, 'You're selling the wrong thing. You're selling fitness when you should be selling this emotion.'" Perlman "wanted to turn Zumba into a brand where people felt that kind of free and electrifying joy." He figured out from the facial expressions of people enjoying the movement that selling Zumba with images of "electrifying joy" instead of pain would not only inspire the question "How do you want to feel?" but it would inspire a lot more people to seek a workout where fun and feeling didn't exist in contradiction with one another.

Nothing worth having comes easy.

We have an obsession with hustle culture, with the allure of punitive progress, and with the notion that sacrifice is a sexy—and even necessary—part of someone's story. When I was in the military in Australia, this approach was a big part of how higher-ranked officers would motivate us. They would plant the idea in our heads that if we kept doing more of the boring or undesirable postings, then one day we would get our dream post. Earning a promotion in rank was always tied to misery, which, to be quite honest, instilled in me a distrust in anything that came naturally.

And when I got to the root of what was going on there, a much darker question came to mind. Was it possible that the military fostered this toxic mentality deliberately to confuse our understanding of what I would one day come to know as Intentionality?

Looking back, I believe that sacrificing and suffering were being sold to us as an intention. We were being indoctrinated. We were being coded to believe that the physical nature of living with intention and pursuing a virtuous goal would mean feeling like shit. In their eyes, feeling like shit meant you were doing something right.

For me, this was actually one of the more jaw-dropping connections I'd made. If I was trained to believe that success could not exist without sacrifice and that worth could only come from hardship, how could I ever fully trust or experience the feeling of inner peace?

Time heals all wounds.

As human beings, the fact that we have finite time on Earth may be our biggest incentive to live fuller, more meaningful lives. We know we only get one life. We know that life, in comparison to the vast stretch of the universe, is very short. These are not novel musings. The passage of time is one of the few certainties we have in this universe, so it has always confused and befuddled me when human beings are quick to blurt out the mantra that time is going to heal us. If anything, time is going to end us.

Time is not a one-size-fits-all remedy. It assumes that we all have the gift of more time—and we don't. Some of us are sick, and some of us are taken in a moment's flash. The assumption that time can pass in favor of our well-being is just something we tell ourselves to avoid the truth that feeling before healing is a must.

If time healed all wounds, then why are so many full-blown adults in therapy talking about their past as if it happened yesterday?

And when we say "wounds," what we mean is trauma. In his pioneering book *The Body Keeps the Score: Brain, Mind, and Body in the Healing of Trauma*, Bessel van der Kolk, M.D., details a 1994 study he and his colleagues at Massachusetts General Hospital completed to examine how people recall trauma.

The study was an intimate look at the difference between normal and traumatic memory. Van der Kolk and his colleagues revealed that "weddings, births, and graduations were recalled as events from the past, stories with a beginning, middle, and end" and that "nobody said there were periods when they'd completely forgotten any of these events." But "the traumatic memories were disorganized." They found that the study's participants "remembered some details all too clearly (the smell of the rapist, the gash in the forehead of a dead child) but could not recall the sequence of events or other vital details (the first person who arrived to help, whether an ambulance or a police car took them to the hospital)."[3]

One thing that has particularly fascinated me about this study is that the participants' relationship with their memories of trauma changed over time. Van der Kolk and his co-authors found that "the five [participants] who said they had been abused as children had the most fragmented narratives—their memories still arrived in images, physical sensations, and intense emotions."

Van der Kolk believes the study confirmed that "traumatic memories are fundamentally different from the stories we tell ourselves about the past" and that "the different sensations that entered the brain at the time of the trauma are not properly assembled into a story . . . "[4] Reading this has quite frankly helped to validate both my personal experiences with trauma and my criticism of the mantra.

For a long time, I could tell you about the details of my parents' room, the way the rain looked pouring on our house, and even how everything smelled the day I began disassociating from my father. I could recall a hardening in me because of the wounds inflicted, but my memories arrived in fragments that I once described as the perfect storm, one with lasting damage, discord, and hubris. My ability to heal from this was always clouded by my inability to revisit trauma without reliving it to my detriment. How could time heal my wounds when I was processing them through a lens that tended to distort chronology and context as a mechanism of self-preservation?

When it comes to my own history with abuse, I had long been conditioned to believe that the passage of time—especially when paired with talking about my trauma—would miraculously result in some kind of healing. This idea was so ingrained in me that at a certain point, I think I expected it to just happen. And when that healing remained elusive, I started to feel like a failure. And that's how I felt for a long time.

As van der Kolk wrote, "Perhaps the most important finding in our study was that remembering the trauma with all its associated effects, does not, as Breuer and Freud claimed back in 1893, necessarily resolve it. Our research did not support the idea that language can substitute for action."

Despite the fact that the people who say time heals all wounds are likely very well intentioned in their effort, ironically, there is very little intention behind the words themselves. Time doesn't do anything but tick forward. It's what we do with it that makes the difference.

Last, this mantra is a product of a culture obsessed with healing. We are consumed with fixing ourselves—when in reality we need to be focused on feeling our emotions fully and processing them in real time. Because feeling before healing is paramount.

What doesn't kill you makes you stronger.

Despite Kelly Clarkson's best efforts to further popularize Nietzsche's saying in her 2011 chart-topping single, "What Doesn't Kill You (Stronger)," I'm still unconvinced it's an effective maxim. Even with Clarkson's heartfelt personal attachment to it, I've always had concerns that it bifurcates the complex nature of the human experience. Because sometimes what doesn't kill us breaks us in ways other than death—in prolonged, painful ways that require more than just the binary assumption that surviving is enough.

Strength is subjective, but strength is also circumstantial. And while one of the core tenets of my teachings is taking radical ownership of your circumstances, Intentionality can only be navigated by first acknowledging the uncomfortable truths about inequality and the context needed to better address it.

In the United States, perhaps one of the most horrific examples of this mantra being taken to the extreme is in our system of mass incarceration. According to the Prison Policy Initiative, the United States incarcerates 664 people for every 100,000 residents.[5] With 25 percent of the world's incarcerated population, a country founded on the idea of liberty and justice for all has become the most unnecessarily punitive nation in the world. We have developed a multisystemic trap devoid of compassion, rehabilitation prospects, and educational and economic tools for empowerment. When you take a closer look at these injustices, you will see that the systems that perpetuate incarceration were designed to test the strength in the most vulnerable among us.

David Hawkins long espoused the importance of context versus content. He condemned the ongoing proposition of solutions without adequately accounting for the context of what created the present challenges. Hawkins said, "To fail to properly contextualize content has historically been the basis for the slaughter of millions of people in every century throughout human history. To ignore context is the greatest source of catastrophe for every generation of man, and it continues on in the present time with the same catastrophic consequences."[6]

Dr. Rosemarie Allen, an early childhood education expert known for her work trying to upend "the preschool-to-prison pipeline," helps us to have a deeper context of how our systems run and how urgent transformation must be implemented.

In her TEDxMileHigh talk, she explained that children "who are suspended are ten times more likely to enter the juvenile justice system."[7] This is one of the cold, hard truths about the systems both within us and around us—negativity begets negativity.

Dr. Allen also quoted John Herner, former president for the National Association of State Directors of Special Education, who famously said, "When children don't know how to read, we teach; when they don't know how to write, we teach; when they don't know how to ride a bike, we teach. But, when children don't know how to behave, do we teach, or do we punish?"

Dr. Allen continued, "Imagine a world where we intentionally taught children prosocial skills, gave them many opportunities to practice, and positively reinforced them every time they used those skills."

I love this. She has not only provided the context for our current situation, but most importantly she has made the case for creating new content. She says it right there—imagine a world with intention! I don't know about you, but I'd rather imagine that and then build it than settle for a mantra that cycles future generations through negative belief loops and systems in perpetuity.

Work harder than you think you did yesterday.

As we've discussed, we are coded into a world where work is often our main identity. So we are conditioned to think that if our workday isn't all-consuming, it somehow isn't enough. This adage is plagued with thought distortion about how much or how little output we have already made. In one sentence it manages to insult our ability to estimate our achievements to date while attempting to shame us into achieving more based solely on that initial level of insecurity. It also reflects how we process a day's work as well as how we value our life's work.

Poet Ocean Vuong told the *Guardian*, "I truly don't believe that a writer should just keep writing as long as they're alive. I see my career not by how much I can produce but by how the work can get me to where I can meaningfully stop and be satisfied with what I've done. I'm more interested in stopping well rather than endlessly creating."[8]

Vuong taps into something that in today's world seems almost counterintuitive. For him, the lens of achievement cannot come from anything other than what he refers to as "satisfying the artistic potential within oneself." In other words, he is working for how he feels—not for what the critic, the audience, or anyone else for that matter, believes he should achieve with his creative endeavors.

We could all venture to mimic Vuong's approach of conforming less, feeling more, and finding ourselves in the process.

When the going gets tough, the tough get going.

This was one of my father's go-to gems. But it implies that the people who rise to the occasion are the strongest and that anyone who doesn't meet the moment is weak or less than.

Even though it is what we heard, I don't believe my father intended to imply that we were weak by default if we weren't tough. But I do believe he was the product of a generation that frowned upon vulnerability and placed greater value on physicality and determination in young boys than it did on emotional intelligence.

The result of that value making its impression in our home was an unspoken culture of fear and an ongoing, persistent field of negative energy. We never knew what side of our dad we were going to get, so we certainly never knew if we needed to toughen up or get going.

And then there's my personal favorite . . .

People don't change.

The thing is—that's not true of all people. It's not true of me, and I suspect it is not true of you either.

And anyone who perpetuates this myth is somebody who has no vested interest in breaking the cycle of absolutes, and who believes they will find far greater safety in staying the same than they would in meaningful change.

Whether it was from a teacher, my father, a military officer, or one of those aspirational signs with the terrible fonts, these sayings were everywhere I turned. For years I never questioned these so-called nuggets of wisdom.

But that's just it. They were not and are not words of wisdom.

In the end, more than anything else, they are just things that people say not because they genuinely believe them or because they feel good to say, but simply because people think they should. And it doesn't matter whether these sentiments are mindlessly or maliciously repeated, because the result is always the same.

It took me nearly three and a half decades to figure these patterns in language out. I encourage you to start now: Question the origin and intention of what is being said to you and the phrases you repeat. This is a wonderful start to better understanding the coding at your core. So look back and come to terms with the fact that any blind adherence to these stubborn, deeply rooted linguistic programs that may have been running within you likely does not serve you. And when you are able to acknowledge that, you'll then be able to identify and accept what language is encouraging your negative belief loops, and what specifically in your life is ripe for change.

Illusion

If I ask you to tell me the first thing that comes to mind when I utter the word *illusion*, what does that bring up for you?

A few years back, my first reaction probably would have been to envision an optical illusion like a heat mirage or perhaps even a magic trick that stumped me. But an illusion is rarely only ever about something as external as trick of sight. More than anything, it's about feelings. And in particular, it's about misguided feelings.

When Sarah and I moved from Australia to the United States, we were taking a marked departure from the people we were supposed to be and the lives we were expected to lead. We believed that *when* we got to America and removed ourselves from the sudden loss of Sarah's father—and *when* we were finally in a home of our own—we would feel fulfilled. We would feel happy.

We loved Colorado and were excited about the idea of moving to Beaver Creek, a premier Colorado ski destination, because we knew that when we moved, we would have access to skiing 100 days or more each year, and we would be building a life of adventure that would belong to the both of us.

But *when* is a four-letter word.

When has gotten me into a lot of trouble over the years.

Because *when* is an illusion.

As it turned out, I did get more than 100 days of skiing in, and we did build a life of many mountain adventures. We hiked, camped, white water rafted, and hosted friends in our luxurious home. But at the end of the day, all the things we'd fantasized about fulfilling us or making us happy couldn't outweigh the inconvenient feelings we'd pushed aside—out of habit, out of coding, and out of naive hopes for a better future.

In his book *Happier: Can You Learn to Be Happy?*, Harvard-trained psychologist Tal Ben-Shahar coined the phrase "arrival fallacy." According to him, the "arrival fallacy is this illusion that once we make it, once we attain our goal or reach our destination, we will reach lasting happiness."[9]

Like so many others, I am not immune to this fallacy. Just look at how I talked about our move—as if moving to America was somehow going to remedy the wounds within us as individuals and as a couple. It's not to say that joy was not found along the way. It was. But what I am saying is that while not uncommon, my presumption that *when* would be a turnkey, fix-all mantra for true happiness was fairly shortsighted.

We have all become comfortable with the illusion of *when* because it allows us to not deal with any of the uncomfortable feelings or challenges that may come up now. But I'm going to let you in on a secret.

When it comes to *when*, there are only two realities and it's also possible, if not likely, that you have experienced or are experiencing them concurrently.

Reality #1: *When* is usually a disappointment.

It comes but it certainly doesn't deliver. You expected it to give you a feeling that you probably weren't even clear on. But unfortunately, because you were relying on something to happen to you or for external conditions to change, you didn't make a full connection with yourself. And a full connection with yourself is the only way to achieve true happiness. This disappointment occurs repeatedly because human beings spend a lot more time fantasizing about what we want happiness to *look* like rather than what we want happiness to *feel* like.

A 2019 *New York Times* article that further examined Ben-Shahar's arrival fallacy also takes a look at its connection to Dr. Jamie Gruman's research around affective forecasting. Dr. Gruman, University of Guelph senior research fellow and professor says, "Affective forecasting is our ability to predict how events will make us feel." He points out that "we tend to be pretty good at knowing what things are going to make us happy and unhappy, but we're not very good at predicting the intensity and the duration of the effect of events."[10]

What this means is that even if what we achieve is precisely in line with what we have on our vision boards, because we have only correlated our happiness with an external reward, we are only able to feel it for a finite period of time—and even then, we can't truly know if it will meet our needs.

Reality #2: *When* may never come.

The dreams you have are consistently on the horizon but often feel outside of your reach, which means that the happiness you associate with those dreams remains at a distance.

How often have we heard the story of an overworked spouse or parent who makes promises they can't keep with their partner or child? How often have we been that person who says, "As soon as I finish this deal, I'll be home more," or, "As soon as I make more money, we'll be able to take that trip"?

The answer is: too often. It's so often that over time, we aren't just worn down, but we wake up thinking, *Where did my life go? How much time or energy have I wasted thinking this way?* That's because we are so far removed and disconnected from how we pictured happiness to be that we lose the sense of intention and urgency needed to prioritize it. And unfortunately, we often disillusion others in the process.

So try to remember that the setbacks from spending too much of your existence living with illusion are substantial. And yes, at the heart of your operating system may be a persistent arrival fallacy, a flimsy affective forecasting model, a tank with false hope, and a deeply embedded misinterpretation of true happiness. But guess what? That's okay. Because when you realize what shapes you at your core and what has been inherent in how you process the life you lead, this is where the shift truly begins. And when it comes to the journey that you are taking right now, I'd love it if you could just do me—and yourself—one small favor. Remove the illusion of *when* by focusing more on being fulfilled in your present reality, and I promise you won't just see, but you'll feel the lasting difference.

Information

When is also a big part of the illusion with breaking news. In fact, when something big happens, something that demands national or international coverage, that's when our negative belief loops hit us with their highest velocity and veracity. That's when all the plates are spinning, when all the effort in the world is being made to frame the story of the world through what is broken, rather than through what can be done to fix it. And when that news breaks, our ability to consume it and intentionally respond to it is at its most vulnerable.

Chris Hayes, the host of MSNBC's *All In with Chris Hayes*, recently said on X (formerly Twitter), "There's an old saying in newsrooms that 'we don't cover the planes that land,' which is to say that the news runs on crisis and disaster and bad things happening unexpectedly and not things slowly getting better, and yet . . . "[11]

He's right.

According to Betsi Grabe, a well-known media scholar whose work focuses on the influence of media images upon people's understanding of the world around them, "Compelling negativity is the most persistent news selection principle—over time, across cultures, and despite damning criticism."[12]

This is, of course, not to say that there are not negative things happening in the world, or that we do not need to be aware of the world around us. Nor is questioning information an invitation to discount the need for good journalists who maintain objectivity and who pursue truth and accountability. And media skepticism is also not a permission slip to embrace the idea that ignorance is bliss (another incredibly unproductive metaphor many of us have subscribed to). If anything, acknowledging the negative news filter as yet another pervasive belief loop spinning within our world and subsequently within ourselves is a wake-up call for finally understanding the breadth of our coding.

The world is a complex, never-ending series of systems breaking down and regenerating at all times, and news is being made in every second of every hour of every day, in every corner of the world. But the way that news is packaged and distributed often leaves little room for a nuanced understanding of current events, let alone any ability to learn from the past.

Much like the magnetic nature and efficacy of negative language, this cycle persists because the people responsible for contextualizing and distributing today's information are doing so out of habit. Just as we've all picked up language, illusions, and bad habits from our upbringing, we've picked up negative habits with respect to the evolving information age from our predecessors as well.

Story editors, executive producers, reporters—these people, even with the best-laid plans, only have so much landscape across which to disseminate their information in an organized, coherent way. Naturally, when it comes to providing deeper detail and context, they must make cuts. And these cuts impact what we are exposed to.

Consider Lisa Feldman Barrett's argument: "The human brain is structured to learn many different concepts and to invent many social realities, depending on the contingencies it is exposed to. This variability is not infinite or arbitrary; it is constrained by the brain's need for efficiency and speed, by the outside world, and by the human dilemma of getting along versus getting ahead."

Barrett concludes, "Your culture handed you one particular system of concepts, values, and practices to address that dilemma."[13] This is particularly accurate if you apply it to the medium of news. As human beings, we are structured to navigate and even seek complexity, but the system tasked with providing us information serves it in reductive portions often in direct contradiction with our bandwidth for learning.

Limits on how diverse a lens we're given through which to learn is just one of the problems. Our emotions also take a hit from the cyclical nature of and penchant for negativity in the news. Have you ever heard the nickname "the outrage machine" for cable news or social media? Critics gave the media that name for a reason. In the U.S., it can feel like it's designed to lock us into a vicious cycle: one where the more media we consume, the angrier we are—and the angrier we are, the more media we consume. As a result, the more information we acquire, the less Intentionality we retain.

Think back to the last time you read an article or watched a clip about something happening in the world. How did you feel afterward? Not about the story itself, but about *having read* the article or *having watched* the clip?

When we mindlessly consume information through only a negative lens, we fail to make a deeper, necessary connection between what we absorb and how we feel as a result of that absorption. This means that if the curators of the information industry are out of touch with humanity, then the most intentional first steps we can take are to consume with greater consciousness.

The world has effectively monetized the consumption of negative information by ensuring that you leave that interaction feeling a certain way—that you feel like informing yourself was a good deed, where the act of accumulating information is equated with helping to solve the problem in the story itself. Now, don't get me wrong. Good journalism can effectively translate awareness to action, and it is good to be aware. But more often than not, we see performative retweets and clickbait activism—all behaviors that feed right back into the habits and the cycle of negativity, further compounding our coding with stronger negative belief loops and programming.

Think about the military-industrial complex. When I was contemplating leaving the Australian army, there was a lot of fear around my decision—fear that was a product of the codependency created and upheld by the institution itself. The army made me feel special. It made me feel important. When I was in officer training, the army told me that I wouldn't be able to relate to my friends outside it anymore because I was at a higher level. And then at the same time, if I expressed any interest in a life beyond the ranks, I was told that my skills didn't quite translate to the requirements of the outside world. The formula for retention was essentially to both boost my ego and suppress any desire for leaving the system. Eventually I caught on.

It's far easier—and more profitable—to make someone afraid of something than it is to get them to invest their energy in recoding and restabilizing broken but lucrative systems. In fact, the ecosystem for this feedback loop has one of the most robust psychological infrastructures in the world.

We hear about a major event, often something scary or novel in its threat to us, and we refresh our social media and news feeds for the latest information. This is because when faced with the unknown, we've been conditioned to believe that having more information can protect us from an ongoing threat or danger. The problem with that belief is that it's not always true.

Aza Raskin, the inventor behind the infinite-scrolling feature used on many platforms and social media apps such as X (formerly Twitter) and Instagram, has very vocally apologized for his innovation and the addictions often attributed to it. For what it's worth, I do not believe he knew that especially during a global pandemic, billions of people might hole up with their devices and turn to an activity now commonly referred to as "doomscrolling" (consuming excessive amounts of negative information online). We are losing control of our intake of information and our ability to counteract our deeply embedded loops of fear, or, as Raskin describes the situation, "we are losing control of the tools we created."[14]

While discussing the psychological and emotional impacts of doomscrolling, Dean McKay, a Fordham University professor, said that "terror, when witnessed from the comfort of the viewer's home . . . ha[s] a potentially calming effect." He asserts that people wind up reconciling the dissonance by feeling that "'things are pretty horrible [but] I'm comfortable, so I'm going to be able to sleep well tonight knowing that [I can feel good about] my station in life.'"[15]

This would mean that we are so far down the rabbit hole of functioning with fear that not only are we conditioned to be comforted by it, but we are also conditioned to engage with it without intention. We are led to believe it's a natural part of life to feel fear and self-soothe, rinse, and repeat. But if we allow ourselves to do that, we lose touch with the infinite power of love.

So ask yourself: *What would happen if I approached civic responsibility and the idea of being a global citizen from a place of love?* I mean that genuinely. I know it may sound naive, but consider this: What if having an understanding of the goings-on in the world was far less about a fear of extinction, or about the imprinting of fear to create a misplaced sense of responsibility, and instead was about a civic-minded commitment to—and love for—our fellow beings?

When you can dig deeper and sincerely call into question the collective consumption of information, you can acknowledge not only that the business of fear is perhaps the single biggest threat to living with love, but also that you can play a fundamental role in changing the situation.

Business

Now that we know fear is a feeling that can reap tremendous financial benefits for the news industry, it's critical that we understand how feeling is weaponized in other business operations as well. You may recall that WeWork, the controversial company founded by Adam Neumann, invested billions of dollars in upholding the principles of a kibbutz, inspiring employees to embrace a family-like setting, and in making sure a workplace feels communal. Neumann thought this would incentivize people to not just join, but build a movement. And while Neumann has rightfully fallen under the microscope of investors, and while the model itself was not pandemic proof, the initial idea of selling a workspace for its feeling of community was, at the time, revolutionary—particularly for independent contractors and small business owners looking for camaraderie in a corporate setting.

Airbnb popularized the saying "belong anywhere," because its founders realized that what it was offering was more emotional and experiential than booking a hotel. But this idea of belonging also extended to the employee experience. According to Insider Intelligence,[16] after struggling in the early years of the pandemic, Airbnb was able to make the future of work synonymous with the future of travel, ultimately growing the company's gross profit from $3.6 billion in 2019 to $4.8 billion in 2021.

What's fascinating about this is that by expanding its motto of belonging anywhere when referring to a customer experience to working from anywhere when referring to its employees, Airbnb was able to equate flexibility with a feeling—feeling better about work, travel, convenience—all of it.

These are just two examples of global companies who, like Zumba, figured out that monetizing feelings would put them ahead of the curve. But even so, the corporate landscape has been inconsistent, at best, in how it values or devalues the power of feeling.

A 2014 Gallup poll found that more than half of workers in America defined themselves based on their jobs.[17] And while we could certainly attribute much of this to the fact that since this country's founding we have tied the idea of the American dream to *how much* we are willing to work, this poll illustrates that we also attach much of our identity to *how* we earn a living.

Professor Amy Wrzesniewski, then at Yale, taught that this is also related to how we see our value in the larger collective; that what we do professionally is "symbolic of the things [we] care about . . . symbolic of [our] offering to the world."[18]

I think we can all relate to what Wrzesniewski and the poll reveal. I know that when selling my first business turned out to be far less lucrative than I'd envisioned, I felt it was a reflection not only of my work ethic, but also of what others thought my company was worth to the world. I was directly correlating both the value of the sale and the net worth of my company with my own self-worth. And it was natural for me to make this correlation—I had become so entrenched in my business, in how much time, energy, and passion I'd invested in it, that any undervaluation felt personal. And that's because the business world at large has intentionally fostered a society where our worth is measured by our work.

But I want you to stop for a second and think about what has happened when you've faced a challenge or crisis at work. My situation was less common in that I was my own employer—yet even then, I was still left with feelings of unworthiness. But what about you? What about a job you have, or had in the past, where you answer(ed) to someone else? Did you ever express an idea that your company didn't use? How about when an outcome or resolution didn't land in your favor? Have you ever needed a vacation or personal day that felt inconvenient to a superior? Were you supported? Or were you immediately questioned about your dedication, loyalty, or commitment to the mission of the company? Or worse yet, when disappointed or facing an impasse during a challenge in the workplace, have you been met with the familiar, frustrating trope, "Don't take it personally—it's just business"?

I have—and I imagine, at some point, you've experienced versions of these as well.

Let's break it down.

A work environment that highlights community and feelings of togetherness when they incentivize toxic work-life boundaries or when it can boost a brand's story, yet villainizes emotion when it's a convenient bogeyman to the bottom line—that's by design. And in many ways, our collective fogginess, our weariness about showing emotion and whether our "feelings" will be valued or dismissed on the job, is a protective mechanism that maintains this hostile design.

Furthermore, organizational and financial overviews of what it means to be human can often miss the mark. According to psychology professor Lisa Feldman Barrett, Ph.D., economists have, at times, oversimplified the human brain. In her book *How Emotions Are Made*, Barrett points out that according to these economists,

"Mathematical models indicate that under certain conditions, unregulated free-market economies do work well. But one of those 'certain conditions' is that people are rational decision makers."[19]

The problem is that these economists are employing absolutes, false choices, and false equivalencies. And they're getting it wrong when it comes to some of the biggest financial crises of our generation.

Their presumption is that the opposite of "rational and work-focused" is "emotional."

Emotions continue to be framed as the enemy of a sound economy, the enemy of a flourishing business, and generally speaking, a risk to the status quo.

But these assumptions can be costly in more ways than one.

Barrett talks about a "body budget," or the way in which the brain calculates and regulates energy for well-being. She states, "You cannot overcome emotion through rational thinking . . . Even when you experience yourself as rational, your body budget and its links to affect are there, lurking beneath the surface."[20]

Human beings are wired to function with feelings front and center. Barrett points to the Western myth that "the human mind is a battlefield where cognition and emotion struggle for control of behavior"—and that the word we use to describe ourselves as insensitive or rash is *thoughtless*, which "connotes a lack of cognitive control." [21]

Rolled right into the traditional lexicon of how we talk, see, buy, act, consume, and communicate with each other is this binary fight between feeling and thinking—a fight that, if you ask me, has no business being fought in the first place. Both are native to our human systems. So why are they being pitted against each other instead of encouraged to function in concert?

In his many experiments and studies of human behavior and instinctive feelings, psychologist Gerald L. Clore explored how gut feeling plays a role in decision-making and the phenomenon of "affective realism."[22]

In a 2000 study, Clore and his co-authors concluded that "affect provides constraints on beliefs and vice versa."[23] He also discussed how when we are in love with someone, we tend to believe that they have very positive attributes—but if the relationship goes south, we develop negative beliefs.

In other words, beliefs are calibrated to our experiences and, in his words, are "compatible with internal evidence in the form of feelings."[24]

This is crucial, because economists have not been accounting for the one thing that makes us—us. They have not been accounting for emotion, which means they've often failed to make recommendations that could result in long-term economic success.

We're complex, layered beings. And our feelings cannot be taken out of the equation.

Companies, organizations, and communities are, after all, made up of humans, so acknowledging that functioning *with* feeling, and not in spite of it, is in everyone's best interest.

I found that this proved especially true when examining my relationship with the team members within my company. In the past, I'd often bring people in and we'd have a good thing going, but I would never fully commit to them. In one of my biggest professional regrets, I would open the dialogue about equity but then not follow through. This understandably created mistrust within the team. My wavering would then validate their fears, which would make them pull away a bit—and then I would wonder if they needed to prove their worth in a greater way. But ultimately what was happening was, I was projecting my own feeling of fear and abandonment—and concurrently expecting team members to go to great lengths to prove to me that they wouldn't leave. This didn't work for obvious reasons, not the least of which is that I exhibited to the people closest to me in the workplace that I didn't trust them.

I was the problem. It was me who pushed them away—not the other way around. I didn't ask for help when I knew my team members were capable of providing it, and then I judged their performance based on the uncompleted tasks I never expressed a need for help with in the first place. I had unwittingly weaponized my fear of abandonment at the expense of my team members and ultimately our ability to maintain collaborative trust in one another. I'm not proud of this chapter of my professional life, but it did teach me firsthand how easily feeling can be taken for granted, underestimated, and misused. Since then, I've made deliberate efforts to ensure that I only make promises I can keep and follow through on, that the people I work with feel supported, and that the workplace I am building appropriately calibrates for feeling as an asset and not a liability.

With the distance I now have from the dissolutions of my companies and my marriage, I've been able to see that the power of negativity around feeling is shaped by the intentional contradictions programmed into our existence. I hope you'll learn from the mistakes I made before I figured that out. And I hope you'll consider that because the world's systems teach you to simultaneously value and suppress the act of feeling, they will, for as long as possible, keep you in a holding pattern—one where you can never fully experience the enormous impact feelings can have on all aspects of your life.

Don't let your negative belief loops threaten the relationships you value the most. Acknowledge that external forces have a tremendous impact on your internal feelings and interface negatively or positively with your operating system.

And then learn to be a person who lives and leads with that self-awareness at the heart of your decision-making. The next circuit breaker, the Nervous System Reboot, will help you to get started on this front.

Circuit Breaker:
Nervous System Reboot

For this next circuit breaker, you're going to practice the 4-7-8 breathing technique. While this technique can be traced back to the ancient yogic practices of pranayama that began in India, you might be familiar with it because Dr. Andrew Weil, a Harvard-trained doctor and pioneer of integrative medicine, brought it further into the mainstream nearly a decade ago, calling it a "natural tranquilizer for the nervous system."[25]

The 4-7-8 breathing rhythm, while often associated with relaxation, can also be used as a focus mechanism. If we can focus on the fact that we may have feelings of judgment or shame associated with the impressions and other external negative belief loops we are learning about here, then we can accept their impact without questioning our ultimate ability to respond to them.

Step One: *Sit upright and place your tongue on the roof of your mouth.*

Find an upright position that feels comfortable and close your eyes. Place your tongue on the roof of your mouth, with the tip near the back of your front teeth. Take a moment to notice what your tongue and the roof of your mouth feel like pressed together.

Step Two: *Open your lips into an O shape and let out all your air for eight counts.*

Gently open your lips, and with your tongue still at the roof, exhale through your mouth for a count of eight. You should be breathing out all the air you can. You will feel a gradual whooshing release through your tongue, teeth, and lips.

Step Three: *Close your mouth and take a gentle breath through your nose for four counts.*

Begin inhaling back in through your nose. Feel your nostrils opening as the air enters.

Step Four: *Hold your breath for seven counts.*

Gently hold your breath at the top of your inhale—not a fierce, tight hold but a soft, small contraction of your nostrils—for a count of seven.

Step Five: *Do four more rounds of this breathing pattern.*

With each round, you will become more and more relaxed, but focused. At first, this will feel a bit mechanical and you'll be ironing out the kinks of what might feel like overthinking your breath. You also may feel lightheaded or off-kilter. That's okay. Keep going and trust the process. You are not overthinking; you are beginning to feel. You are installing a new focus mechanism for the journey ahead. You are soothing your sympathetic nervous system and settling into your body.

Once you've done this breath, you will have experienced firsthand that circuit breakers do more than just empower us to reset. They are a manual override to the complex world of negative coding that exists both within and beyond ourselves.

We are all coded to our very core—coded to buy into stories we didn't write, to believe the wisdom of the crowd, to subscribe to outdated methods of productivity and fulfillment, and to experience a kind of Stockholm syndrome in relationship with the external systems that profit most from our suffering.

But once you learn how these negative belief loops continue to code you and how they shape the way you feel and experience the world, you can also learn what you can do to change course.

KEY TAKEAWAYS

Family

- The question "How do you want to feel?" is more effective than "What do you want?" in moving toward wholeness and inner peace.

- Think back to how you answered the question "What do you want to be when you grow up?" when you were younger. Do you remember what influenced your answer? How have those earlier influences impacted your career journey?

Language

- Language can act as a spell; we are deeply influenced by sayings and clichés that we grow up hearing.

- Identify one of the aforementioned clichés you've heard before and list evidence from your own life that negates it.

Illusion

- Using the term *when* is an act of illusion because it enables you to avoid feeling in the moment. It always results in disappointment and keeps your dreams at a distance.

- Focus on removing *when* from your vocabulary for a day and keep a tally of how often it appears.

Information

- In this evolving information age, the benefits of having access to so much information are often outweighed by our lack of Intentionality in consuming it.

- Identify one thing you can change today to be more intentional with your media intake.

Business

- Companies, organizations, and communities are made up of humans, and humans operate on feelings. Acknowledging that our feelings are our greatest assets, especially in the workplace, is in everyone's best interest.

- Try the 4-7-8 breathing technique the next time you are feeling stressed or overly stimulated in your workplace and notice the fast-acting effect it can have on soothing your sympathetic (fight-or-flight) nervous system. Maybe even invite your colleagues to join along with you!

Part III

RECODING

As you sow in your subconscious mind,
so shall you reap in your body and environment.

—JOSEPH MURPHY

CHAPTER 6

REPETITION

Repetition is key for recoding the subconscious mind because it leverages the brain's capacity for neuroplasticity, which is the ability of the brain to form and reorganize synaptic connections in response to experience. The subconscious mind is deeply influenced by repeated thoughts, behaviors, and feelings, and this is where the power of repetition comes into play.

Let's look at examples of things you likely do in your everyday life. Tying your shoelaces, driving a car, riding a bike, and brushing your teeth are a few. You practiced these, and one day, they just clicked—which means that your subconscious took over and created a program you are able to repeat. In short, the subconscious is fulfilling its job and saving you energy by doing these things on autopilot.

Autopilot can be an asset or a liability. In the army, it was the way we learned everything. The act of repetition to initiate our autopilot mode was so deeply ingrained and programmed into us that we could probably have performed orders in our sleep. In fact, if you asked me today how to describe in detail an Austeyr rifle, I wouldn't be able to tell you all the different parts, but if you put it into my hands, I'd know exactly what to do with it. And then there's the autopilot I've developed with sweets. I've trained my body to believe that it needs sweets after every meal. The urge comes up, and even though I'm full, I'm still convinced I need to have just one sweet morsel. The next thing you know, because of this conditioning, I'm having multiple treats each day.

Whether it serves you or not, whatever you repeat enough is eventually accepted by your subconscious mind as the truth. This is because your subconscious mind does not distinguish between something that is physically real and what you have felt to be real through your imagination. What you believe and assume to be true is what the subconscious mind accepts as real and what it sets out to create. Your current circumstances will reveal the core beliefs of your personal operating system. We all have persistent negative belief loops that act on autopilot; they operate on repeat without us ever attempting to interrupt them. But repetition works both ways.

With Intentionality, the act of repetition can also be used to create positive belief loops. Your subconscious is a servant of your conscious mind, and as such, whatever the conscious lets in, the subconscious then creates a belief loop around it. This means that when harnessed successfully, repetition is one of the most effective ways for you to optimize your coding.

In this section, you'll learn to create formidable positive belief loops that will enable you to embrace what I've coined the five key intentions of Intentionality. These intentions counteract the most common negative belief loops I have identified pervading the thousands of people I've worked with. The intentions are:

- Leverage energy over time
- Embrace discipline over rigidity
- Choose love over fear
- Practice presence over comparison
- Prioritize feelings over outcomes

Repetition around these five key intentions will help you counter your destructive patterns, abandon the coding that no longer serves you, and pave your own path forward.

Leverage Energy over Time

How many times a day do you think about time? Too many to count, I'm sure.

Time is the standard metric for how we prioritize what is important to us. It's at the core of how we measure the history and strength of our relationships, how we attempt to structure a healthy work-life balance, and how we attempt to make meaning of our existence here on Earth.

But the acceptance of time as the metric for measuring success, credibility, loyalty, effort, and more is a myth. It's a negative belief loop long overdue for an override.

Let's look at an American standard and the common iteration of this loop—the myth of the socially accepted 40-hour work week. Right now, different legislatures and businesses are exploring changing the standard work week to four days or 32 hours. Researchers are citing experiments during the pandemic where productivity did not decrease when employees worked with the motivation of a four-day week. In fact, at Microsoft Japan, researchers found that operating under this structure led to a 40 percent increase in productivity.[1]

Similarly, after a study showed promising results with fewer hours in the workplace, lawmakers in Maryland proposed a bill[2] with hefty tax breaks—one that would incentivize companies to implement the four-day work week going forward.

And this is where we can expect the tentacles of cognitive bias to take hold. When change unfolds, there is always a group of people who simplify their understanding of it by looking at it only through the lens of their personal experiences and preferences.

Change, for them, feels like a criticism of how they've conducted their lives or businesses up until this point. In reality, all the people pushing for change are simply acknowledging an evolving world, a pandemic, collective burnout, and a number of other factors that support the notion that just because something has always been done a certain way doesn't mean it should keep being done that way.

I get it. It's natural to feel discomfort with change. And on a basic level, I understand the intuitive nature of looking at work through the lens of time—time away from our family, friends, and kids, or time we might be giving to a job that's not a passion but something that pays the bills.

But it wasn't until I shifted my metric and opted to intentionally leverage my energy over my time that I began to experience a noticeable uptick in my quality of life.

The executives and leaders I work with often tell me about the stress they experience when having to attend a meeting they don't think they have time for, aren't in the mood for, or don't feel inspired by. I don't say to them, "It's better not to go in there and waste everyone's time," because what going in there would do is far more selfish and unproductive than wasting others' time. You know what I tell them?

I tell them to stop looking at it like they're managing a Google calendar and turn inward for the answers. I tell them, "Look, if you're not in a good energetic place, don't go into that meeting. It's better to cancel it than go in and have your negative energy disrupt that setting. *You're wasting their energy if you do so.*"

A company functions as a battery source. Its leader is the supercharger. What the leader brings or doesn't bring into the room ripples across everyone else. It can either replenish or drain them. After we're able to make that change in how leaders feel about their role and realize how important the personal accountability of their energy is, we can develop an efficient strategy that prioritizes energy.

I hear it time and time again, "I don't have a second to even breathe; I'm back-to-back with meetings." Meetings are one of the stressors my clients mention most—especially because our inner monologue around them is already so dire. Even the thought of a meeting can drain us. The calendar invite comes, and we're already sucked into the idea of how we could better be using our time, right? We conduct meetings out of habit, because we've been programmed to equate frequency with efficiency. This couldn't be more off base.

Arthur C. Brooks's article "Meetings Are Miserable" in *The Atlantic* cited an estimate from software company Atlassian that unnecessary meetings waste $37 billion in salary hours a year. Brooks also posits the idea that the "real problem with meetings is not lack of productivity—it's unhappiness." He suggests that "excessive and unproductive meetings can lower job satisfaction for several reasons," including "increased fatigue" and "surface acting" during the gathering.[3]

Through the lens of Intentionality, this means excessive meetings result in more negative feelings and less productive output.

According to Brooks, surface acting consists of "faking emotions that are deemed appropriate." It is an incredibly concerning development for the future of work. Let me just say, as someone imparting experience and advice rooted in a feelings-first approach to living and leadership, forced or fake feelings are not what you want in yourself or your team members. And if that's where you or your team are at, what's transpiring is likely far more performative than productive.

And the effects aren't just psychological. That "increased fatigue" takes a physical toll on us as well. When we're just sticking around for what amounts to a head count or an infinite to-do list of office meetings or Zooms mandated by C-suite execs, we're far more likely to increase our stress, resentment, and even the risk to our bodies themselves.

More than 50 million Americans live with chronic pain[4]—a number exacerbated by the time spent at home computers and offices in suboptimal postural positions.[5]

This is an incredibly important point we must continue to explore, especially if we consider that ineffectual, old adage that "time heals all wounds." In this instance, time is literally causing, not healing, our wounds. But when we commit to this new perspective, when we make the shift to leveraging energy over time, we are able to relieve the physical impact it has on us.

Another example of how this shows up in the workplace is the uniquely human obsession with resilience. In the corporate world, we often glorify the story of the CEO who sleeps three hours a night and hasn't changed their shirt in days. We idolize the hustle and the persistence of the exhausted—and for what?

In 2018, Elon Musk told the *New York Times* that he worked 120-hour weeks to hit Tesla production goals.[6] This is a habit he notoriously repeated when he purchased Twitter in 2022 and encouraged staffers to sleep at the company's headquarters to meet his metrics for success.

Tim Cook tweeted, "Got some extra rest for today's event. Slept in 'til 4:30."[7] The replies included a lot of supporters saying things like "#teamnosleep," "What it takes to succeed Steve Jobs," and "#Boss."

Do I want to abide by these metrics of success? Definitely not. There's something deeply unsettling about the *Fast Company* issue put out every year with a photo of someone in a suit and a cover article titled, "The Secrets of the Most Productive People." To me they are just reinforcing a collective negative belief loop around the obsession of productivity.

Consider this question: Is there a difference between pain and suffering? Or to take it from another angle, can you define *suffering* without using the word *pain*?

Pain is discomfort—but it can be felt, processed, and learned from. Suffering is unnecessary and avoidable distress. And often it implies that a person is enduring pain much longer than is appropriate or needed. We often equate suffering and hardship with worth—which means that by proxy, we associate time with not just suffering, but success. The longer we suffer, the longer we endure something, the more we have earned the right to claim its rewards.

Unfortunately, with this metric and its corresponding negative belief loop, by the time we've reached our supposed goals, we're too exhausted to enjoy them.

An example of this is the hard-driving work ethic that is way too common in the start-up world. A few years back, the partner in a private equity firm asked me to work with a CEO of one of the tech companies it was invested in. He was worried about her overall health and how it would impact the company's performance.

The CEO was working 16 hours a day with back-to-back meetings. She wasn't sleeping because she was so stressed. She wasn't spending time with her family, and she was coming into work completely burned out.

Her thinking was that if she didn't involve herself in every little thing, the company would fall apart. And she said what we've all said to ourselves and our loved ones when we're overworked: "I just need to get through this, and it will be better."

We discovered her negative belief was "I am inadequate." The loop was rooted in the habit of using time as the core metric in the management of her own life and the workplace's culture.

Negative Belief Loop

FEELINGS
stressed
conflict
exhausted

BELIEF
I am inadequate

BEHAVIORS
focusing on time
and lack of it

THOUGHTS
I just need to get
through this and it
will be better

But her desired feelings were quite different. This woman wanted to feel better. She wanted to feel supported, nourished, and energized. So her positive belief became "I can trust." Her positive thoughts were that she had a team of capable people and that when she took care of herself, she showed up better for others.

Positive Belief Loop

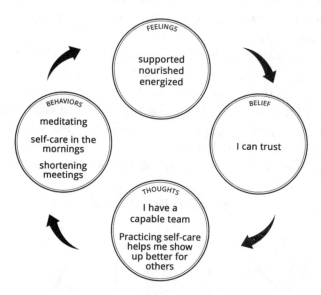

FEELINGS

supported
nourished
energized

BELIEF

I can trust

THOUGHTS

I have a
capable team

Practicing self-care
helps me show
up better for
others

BEHAVIORS

meditating

self-care in the
mornings

shortening
meetings

I even joked with her about the Zen proverb that says, "You should sit in meditation for 20 minutes every day—unless you're too busy; then you should sit for an hour." She discovered that when we meditate, our focus shifts to our energy. With meditation we become more aware, more present, and we are less likely to get lost in negative belief loops, which means we'll make better and more efficient decisions, effectively collapsing the time we previously needed to achieve the very same thing.

At the root of the CEO's misplaced priorities, we found the uncomfortable reality that's true for a lot of us—we aren't strapped for time. We're strapped for energy. The CEO started making all internal and external meetings 15 minutes or less as the standard—and she did an hour of self-care each morning before using her phone.

And the result of creating her own positive belief loop and applying the methods of Intentionality? She achieved what she desired—feeling supported, nourished, and energized. And she dramatically improved the achievements of the company. In turn, the private equity partner who had referred me appreciated this—showing you can have both balance and results!

So the repetition we focused on—the loophole to the CEO's negative belief—was implementing behaviors that enabled her to leverage energy over time.

While exploring this intention, you will learn that a binary approach rarely works. Much like my client, you can expect to feel that you're a work in progress. And that's okay, because while you may still have these pesky, pervasive negative belief loops, it's all about coming back to the present to find that point of leverage.

So let's try this energy management concept out, shall we?

Circuit Breaker:
Physiological Sigh

Breathing is energy—and that's not just a buzz phrase. It's scientifically true. We all need oxygen, right? Well, oxygen plus glucose equals energy.

In preparation for your next positive belief loop creation, you're going to maximize your energy by focusing on what's called a "physiological sigh"—which is a form of breathing proven to alleviate stress and anxiety.[8]

The Physiological Sigh is a type of breath that helps regulate the respiratory system and maintain proper levels of oxygen and carbon dioxide in the body. It has also been linked to the release of a neurotransmitter called noradrenaline, which can have a calming effect on the body and help reduce stress and anxiety.[9] This is also a deep breath that occurs naturally in humans and other mammals—you may notice that babies do this in their sleep. The breath pattern is characterized by a double-inhale sequence, with the first inhale being slightly deeper than normal, then a second inhale followed by a brief pause, and then a prolonged exhale.

According to a study from Stanford Medicine, the physiological sigh or "cyclic sighing" can help regulate your mood within five minutes.[10] David Spiegel, M.D., associate chair of the Department of Psychiatry and Behavioral Sciences and director of the Center on Stress and Health at Stanford Medicine, and co-author of the study, says, "What's interesting about the breath is that it's right on the edge of conscious control. . . . Most of the time, breathing is automatic, like digestion, heartbeat, and other bodily functions, but you can very easily take over and control your breath, which then affects your overall physiology and stress response."

Neurobiologist Andrew Huberman, Ph.D., who co-authored the Stanford study with Dr. Spiegel, says, "The double inhale of the physiological sigh 'pops' the air sacs (called alveoli) open, allowing oxygen in and enabling you to offload carbon dioxide in the long exhaled sigh out."[11]

This is a natural response that happens in your body to balance out your levels of carbon dioxide and oxygen—which means you can use this exercise to focus on everything you just learned about leveraging energy over time and to prepare yourself with the best possible footing for your next positive belief loop creation.

Step One: *Position yourself to feel the expansiveness of your body.*

Find a comfortable yet alert standing or sitting position. Make sure your back is straight, shoulders down, and your collarbone open. Start to feel the expansiveness of your body simply by bringing your attention to it.

Step Two: *Take two sharp inhales through your nose.*

Take a sharp inhale through your nose. Take a small pause here—a moment to hold the breath within and do not let any air out. Then take another sharp inhale through your nose.

Step Three: *Exhale long and slow through your mouth.*

Release your breath out through your mouth. This should be a slow, elongated breath. Imagine that anything you have breathed in is a form of unwanted energy or stress. The exhale is your opportunity to release any tension out of your body.

There is no set amount of time for how long you should engage in doing the physiological sigh. Even as few as three rounds of this extended exhaling exercise can have a dramatic impact on your system. Huberman stated, "This is a real time tool that people can deploy anytime, anywhere to reduce stress."[12] I can't count the number of times I've turned to the cyclical sighing process when something is about to blow up my day and I need a physical reminder that energy, not time, is my most preferred and powerful metric. The results are immediate—and the shift in feeling undeniable.

Anytime you want to create a habit, especially with breath, doing it in tandem with an activity you engage in regularly helps cement it in your system faster. This Physiological Sigh can be utilized right when you wake up in the morning, before and after meetings, or anytime you are about to sit down for a meal. Try scheduling this circuit breaker into your calendar a few times a day until it becomes a natural positive intervention to use any time.

Embrace Discipline over Rigidity

Time isn't the only landmine out there.

Oftentimes, people who come to me for coaching think they're looking for a transformation in terms of their work-life balance, but what they're actually looking for is a better understanding of how they operate. Or, in other words, why we as human beings are so wired to deal in extremes.

When people start their Intentionality journey, not only are they at the brink of exhaustion—they're almost always experiencing the negative belief that perfection is desirable in many, if not all, areas of their lives.

Our culture of "shoulds" and our collective agreement that achievements, or bettering our life, are only possible through the lens of "all or nothing" has further perpetuated the myths we hold around rigidity and discipline.

We see this all the time with relationships, religion, diet culture, exercise, and more.

In addition to having this idea of what our day should look like or how our time should be spent, we've been coded by society's pressures around what we should be eating, what our relationships should look like, how much or little we should be working, and whether we should be more or less of something in someone else's eyes.

We've eliminated the spectrum of possibilities for personal or organizational growth by giving in to the idea that we all live our lives at either A or Z—when in reality, the most transformative work happens somewhere in between.

There's a reason why companies continue to update their visions, values, and cultures. The world is always changing, which means structures both within and beyond the workplace must adapt accordingly.

Let me tell you about another client of mine, Sam, the CEO of a large marketing company who I met when he was on the edge of burnout. I observed that on top of dealing with significant work stress, he was consumed by an all-or-nothing pattern of dieting. This led to tremendous self-worth issues and misplaced labels of failure—and to what end?

Well, for him the pursuit was of perfection. His core negative belief was that he was a disappointment. This belief was tied to a pervasive, brutal dieting plan that allowed very little room for flexibility.

Negative Belief Loop

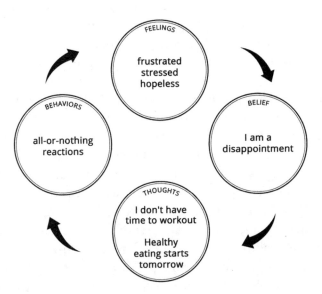

He thought that if he ate poorly in the morning, then he might as well go off the rails for the rest of the day and start his healthy eating regimen the next day. It wasn't a coincidence that on these days, he also thought he didn't have time for a workout. Sam was ending every night shaming himself about the deterioration of his eating throughout the day. He would ruminate on what he could have done differently and criticize himself for never course correcting, and by the time he went to sleep, he felt frustrated, stressed, and hopeless. This was all because not only had he accepted such feelings as a self-fulfilling prophecy, but his subconscious programs were driving his behaviors and quite literally pushing him into a rigid, yet undisciplined pattern.

The simplest way I was able to get through to him was to show him that his behavior was becoming a series of all-or-nothings. In an effort to uncover the intent, I asked, "Why do you want to eat healthy?" I also asked, "Do you think other people have this struggle?" so that we could draw a greater awareness to the fact that he was likely not alone in this uphill battle. And then, in an attempt to take the charge out of Sam making mistakes or less-than-optimal choices, I simply inquired, "Does eating healthier mean you have to eat perfectly?" By digging a little deeper below the surface, I was helping him see that his rigid mindset and the belittling nature of his inner talk were resulting in him reacting to insecurities instead of responding to challenges with intention.

Once we identified how he wanted to feel—empowered, free, and proud—he began to care for himself in more optimal ways and think, *I'm fueling my body with what it needs—and I love and respect my body.* He focused more on how he wanted to feel rather than obsessing over an ideal body weight or shape. He then visualized how he would look and feel as a healthier version of himself. And he started going for short walks throughout the day and journaling about his healthy eating habits. The result? He was able to slow the spinning of his rigid coding—and he was able to create a positive belief loop that zeroed in on the need to believe, and more importantly, feel, that he was already perfect the way he was.

Positive Belief Loop

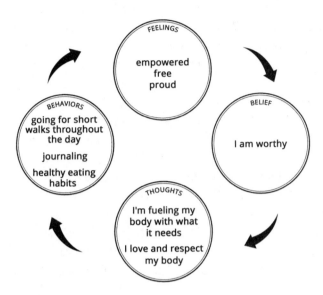

This was so valuable for Sam—and could be an important lesson for you as well. Often, you might think you need an hour of exercise, and if you have only 20 minutes, you don't do it at all because it doesn't reflect your rigid goal. You eat a sugary breakfast, and then you make unhealthy decisions for the rest of the day and call it a wash. You might be living in these extremes—but take a minute to consider that maybe the most fulfilling part of the human experience is a hybrid of many different paths and the result of the incremental steps you make along the way.

Remember Dr. Rosemarie Allen, who worked tirelessly to reverse the impacts of the preschool-to-prison pipeline in the United States? Well, this is precisely what she was getting at. The result of many of the external programs that we've created to try to control our society is a trajectory void of living a more intentional life.

Our perspective on discipline is colored by our experience of it as children. When we do something wrong and are punished, we learn to believe we deserve punishment. We are programmed to believe that discipline goes hand in hand with punishment. Does any of this sound familiar to you?

As a child, I was disciplined through threats and fear—particularly with threats of being slapped or hit with an object. Once for Christmas, I received a wooden spoon in my stocking that was supposed to be a joke, but it imprinted on me, "Be a good boy, or else." Even my Christmas gift wasn't free from the punitive shadow constantly hanging over our house. As I got older, my dad got more creative with his choices. Sometimes there were sticks. One time it was his flip-flops. But my coded takeaway from the experiences was always the same. I had a fundamental understanding that "if I don't do *this*, I'm going to get *that*." It was never about a lesson being learned, and we never sat down to discuss the "why" of anything. In fact, all it ever taught me to do was to figure out new ways to get away with things.

And I didn't keep this kind of behavior compartmentalized for long. At school, I was constantly getting detention. At one point, I had so many detentions to my name that I'd set a school record. Being a troublemaker had become so much a part of my identity that I often accepted the punishment before it even occurred: once, I showed up for detention that I didn't even have. I'd been punished so often that it had become a self-fulfilling prophecy. And it was the same thing at home. Because there was no positive motivation in the threats, especially those with violence, I made it about how much I could get away with until I got the spoon or the stick, or whatever the creative choice of the day was. I figured, why not have fun until the inevitable crackdown?

The fact is that a lot of our programming is written with these kinds of faulty equations. Despite how Sam and I were coded, discipline is not meant to be about punishment at all. Discipline is actually about figuring out what you need to do to best take care of yourself. It's about self-compassion and self-love—and when done right, it is a positive act.

I confided in Sam about my experiences as a kid growing up—and I did this primarily because I wanted him to see that rigidity is what goes hand in hand with punishment, while discipline has nothing to do with it. In fact, the term *discipline* has been hijacked by ill-intentioned people who believe in negative motivation above all else. To combat this conditioning, one of the first steps Sam and I took together was to create a check-in that explored the differences between behaving rigidly and living with discipline. This also included a deeper dive into his specific challenges and where he had developed his programming around punishment:

- Why do you feel you deserve to be punished?

- What is it that you believe you were supposed to do and didn't?

- What have you historically associated the idea of discipline with?

- Where did your assumptions or perceptions around discipline originate?

- What went through your mind when you realized you couldn't do what you set out to do?

- Why is it all or nothing when it comes to eating or exercising?

- Without counting calories or other nutritional metrics, what do you want to feel like after each meal?

When Sam was able to get in touch with the source of his beliefs, thoughts, and behaviors, he finally learned not only to see, but to feel the value in adapting to the circumstances—like fitting in a 20-minute workout when he could. Together we also integrated an easily accessible circuit breaker for the moments where Sam felt his old belief loops were getting the best of him. Funny enough, the override we employed is referred to as the "Perfect Breath."

Trying this circuit breaker would be a great first step for you to deconstruct the desire for perfection and opt instead for dynamic transformation—transformation that comes from embracing discipline and shedding the rigid tendencies of your prior coding that may be stifling your progress.

Circuit Breaker:
The Perfect Breath

This is a simple circuit breaker with minimal instructions. Its purpose is to remind you that no matter what, you are still here, breathing and living. This type of breath has also been referred to as "coherent breathing" because of its mathematical precision as well as its ability to get us into resonance quickly. In this rhythm you breathe in for 5.5 seconds; then you exhale for 5.5 seconds. When you do this, it adds up to 5.5 breaths a minute and the intake of about 5.5 liters of air.[13]

Step One: *Inhale through the nose for five and a half seconds.*

Breathe in through your nose for five and a half seconds. If you cannot do that length of time, that's okay. The counts are not the point. Your presence is the point.

Step Two: *Exhale for five and a half seconds.*

Breathe out through your mouth for five and a half seconds. The consistency, the fact that you are taking a moment to yourself—no matter how long—is the point.

Ironically, the only thing the Perfect Breath requires is your presence—nothing more and nothing less. As you will quickly learn, this is because the Perfect Breath is a circuit breaker that uses a rhythm designed to reinforce the repetition needed for positive belief loop creation. It will quickly put you—and keep you—in not only that rhythmic groove necessary to stay consistent and disciplined about the task at hand, but also to retain self-compassion and the understanding that human progress rarely moves in a straight line.

Choose Love over Fear

Repetition plays an invaluable role in how we can better understand and overcome our fears. One of the body's most fascinating capabilities is within something called the hypothalamic-pituitary adrenal (HPA) axis. This is an internal system that identifies stressors and mediates our responses to them It releases stress hormones and restricts blood cells within our forebrain. It does this because it doesn't want any energy in the conscious mind; instead, it wants us to resort to our natural survival reflexes. It triggers our fight-or-flight responses, such as ensuring we get energy into our legs to quickly escape from a saber-toothed tiger.

But the challenge with this part of our body's makeup is that in the modern-day world, we're not very good at distinguishing threats from nonthreats. And if our limbic system (whose function is to process and regulate our emotions, memories, instincts, and moods) isn't attuned to know the difference in what we perceive as threats, our decision-making abilities can quickly become compromised. For example, if I receive a distressing e-mail, my body activates the same stress response that it would if I were evading a saber-toothed tiger. So my experience of dealing with the e-mail includes restricted blood flow to the conscious mind and a reduced conscious awareness of my physiological response. These reduce my capacity to make an intelligent decision.

Are these two threats at the same level of danger? No. Does my body process both of them based on fears about how or whether I'll be able to handle them? Yes.

I can't tell you the number of times a company has asked me to coach them through a management crisis, and when I get to the core issue, I find the leaders share the conditioned belief that fear is a great motivator.

The truth is, fear is a Molotov cocktail in the decision-making process. Selling it to yourself or your team as an incentive is a fallacy that, if unchecked, will cause destruction within any organization or relationship.

A more specific example of this is a mistake I've personally made as an entrepreneur and witnessed other entrepreneurs experience as well. For months, I'd lived with my hope that a particular employee's understanding of our company's mission would improve—that one day he would wake up and magically be a team player, and we would all live happily ever after. Other employees were unhappy with him, I was unhappy with him, and, as it turns out, he was unhappy too. In fact, he was so unhappy that he quit, set up a competing business, and took clients from us as well. He'd apparently been planning this for quite a while. Had I followed my instincts and taken action on behalf of my team, my company, and myself, we could have avoided the chaos that ensued.

Oftentimes when we have an intuition that a team member isn't the right fit or have evidence that they aren't performing in the way we need them to, we create stories around why we can't let them go. We tell ourselves we haven't made it clear what the company needs from them. We say, "What are we going to do without them? We're going to be down people, and it's going to be hard on the rest of the team."

We create a belief loop built on the hope that if we stay invested in them, it's better for everyone. But really, we're often just afraid of the confrontation.

Because of my fear-based decision-making, I ignored my instincts, overlooked the needs of my team, and set a bad precedent for leadership within the company. My fear of the conversation was driving so much of my decision-making that an entirely new set of casualties developed—casualties that proved far more costly for me, my team, and the company in the long run. On the bright side, the lesson I learned has proved a great cautionary tale for the entrepreneurs I coach today.

When you have to let someone go, it can become not only a source of relief, but also a source of great positivity. Your team will feel clarity. Your team will feel there is accountability. Your team will have structure and an understanding of what's needed. At first it can be difficult for all involved, but inevitably the person at the core of the issue will also feel a sense of freedom and find a path better suited to them.

One time a CEO brought me into her company to help im-prove the culture, strengthen its evolving mission, and navigate the close-mindedness of a legacy CFO. When the CFO was ap-proached with new ideas, the answer was always no before it was yes. His reaction always included some semblance of the notion, "Well, that's the way it's always been done."

The CFO believed change was problematic. He thought, *What if we go over budget? What if I get blamed for a new idea or direction not panning out?* He was a poor listener and certainly not a team player—and his behavior devolved into resistance and defensive-ness. He was working with a single-track mind when it came to any colleagues who pitched or proposed new directions. And ul-timately his fear was stagnating company growth.

Negative Belief Loop

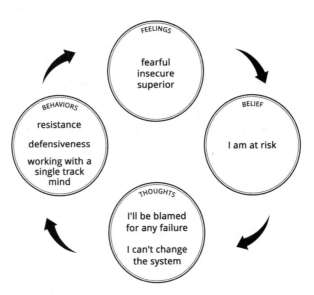

Because the CFO believed that change was not only a threat to his individual job security but also to the company's bottom line, his thoughts and behaviors followed suit. And soon enough, this one individual's fear—and this one individual's negative belief loop—began reverberating until it imprinted on the com-pany itself and became its own belief loop.

Learned helplessness is a clinical theory of what happens when we are conditioned to believe that a situation is out of our control or impossible to change.[14] It's often so deeply rooted in someone, a relationship dynamic, or a company culture that even when opportunities for improvement are readily available, people are unable to utilize those chances.

In the case of this company, the CFO's negative belief loop became a breeding ground for a whole community of learned helplessness. His tradition of no before yes became deeply ingrained in the way that employees killed projects, communicated with one another, or conducted any type of forecasting or innovation. And this cycle in turn created a negative belief loop in the CEO's mind as well. She began fearing that a conversation with the CFO would either end catastrophically or would hurt his feelings—and these were two ends of an emotional pendulum she wasn't interested in swinging. Everyone was resistant to the idea of letting him go.

I helped the CEO come to terms with the reality of the situation and taught her methods to approach this challenge through the lens of love and not fear. We used a reflection to explore the sensitivities around her resistance to confrontation:

- Why are you afraid of talking to the CFO about this long-standing rift within the company?

- Are you being biased about his contributions to the company?

- Are you willing to have a challenging conversation to give him the opportunity to grow with the company?

- Are your fears about hurting his feelings or causing turbulence within the company creating other consequences?

- What would it feel like if you overcame this challenge?

- How can you approach this difficult conversation with love?

I worked with the CEO to help her take ownership of the situation and feel her way out step-by-step. She came to recognize that she was capable of overcoming discomfort and that she was doing what was best for her, the team, and her company. She thought she could compassionately navigate a conversation with the CFO using a feelings-first approach. She chose to demonstrate love over fear and used the Intentionality Communication Method (offered in Part IV of this book) when meeting with him, remembering to use her breath to regulate her reactivity.

For the first time, she was able to feel the exponentially negative impacts of maintaining the status quo and accommodating legacy to avoid confrontation. She realized that the CFO might be set in his ways and that approaching him from a place of love was the only thing left to do. And the result? The conversation went well. Ultimately, though, the CFO wasn't the right fit anymore. Moving forward, the CEO felt more open, more willing to take creative risks, and more optimistic about the future of the company. And what began as an exploration of one leader's negative belief loop culminated in the creation of another leader's positive belief loop.

Positive Belief Loop

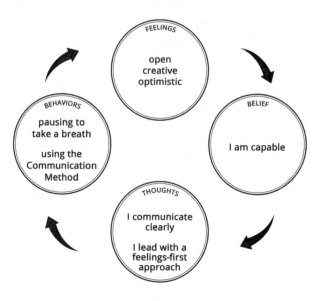

111

Every human being has the potential for change, but the evidence showed that this CFO was unwilling or unable to change in the environment at hand. He was not ready for it, and as such, he was not the right fit for the future the CEO envisioned. By choosing love over fear, this CEO was able to open up a whole new path to leadership—and a whole new experience for her employees.

Learning to choose love over fear certainly isn't a challenge reserved only for the workplace. It's a tug-of-war humans deal with every day of our lives.

When the world offers infinite avenues for a fear-driven existence, choosing love is courageous. The breath is an avenue for you to tap into that courage. It's the way you can access the audacity needed to create and sustain the positive belief loops that eradicate fear and that redefine love as one of the most valuable vantage points in your Intentionality journey.

The Emotional Clearing Breath is specifically designed to help you harness the power of love by coming from a place of acceptance. Not only will it release unnecessary fear loops from your system, it will help you begin to understand your unique relationship with fear.

One thing to be aware of is that you might feel a bit lightheaded, but this is a good sign. In fact, it's a sign that you have changed the equilibrium of the energy circuit and released stagnant energy that no longer serves you. If this happens, take a moment to honor yourself and settle back into normal consciousness, knowing that you are moving energy and recalibrating your system.

Circuit Breaker:
The Emotional Clearing Breath

You can do the Emotional Clearing Breath whenever you identify that you're stuck in a fear loop and can't stop ruminating over a perceived problem. This breath is effective for changing your energy in a relaxed way, simultaneously calming your nervous system.

First, identify a negative feeling that you want to clear with this breathing activity. Think of a recent event or encounter that resulted in you having a negative reaction. See if you can get to the root of what triggered you—not the act itself but what the event activated within you. This will be a core emotion like feeling unworthy, unseen, unlovable, unvalued, inadequate, insignificant, helpless, or rejected.

Here's what will be happening throughout the process on both an energetic and physiological level:

You'll be decompressing the energy that has built up in your system, preparing yourself for the creation of new belief loops, bringing more spirit into your body, and ultimately returning to a state of love.

You'll engage in diaphragmatic breathing. This means filling the belly like a balloon and deepening the breath into the lungs on the inhale, then emptying the lungs and slightly contracting the belly to release air on the exhale. When you consciously do diaphragmatic breathing, you activate the vagus nerve. The vagus nerve is the longest nerve in your body, running from your brain to your large intestine. It activates the parasympathetic nervous system, lowering your heart rate and blood pressure, resulting in you feeling more peaceful. It helps combat any fight-or-flight response activated from the sympathetic nervous system.

You'll take big, deep breaths in through the nose while restricting the throat. This will result in an oceanic-sounding breath. You'll then exhale the air out your mouth, keeping the restriction of your throat and maintaining the oceanic sound— as if you're fogging up a mirror with your breath.

You'll do three rounds of this breath, and then on the fourth exhale, you'll release with a harmonic "O" tone.

Let's begin.

Step One: *Place your right hand on your lower abdominal region and your left hand on your heart. Inhale through your nose.*

As you inhale, feel your breath traveling into your belly with the right hand and then expanding into the left hand on your heart. Focus your awareness on your fear loop: identify the negative feeling you're resisting.

Step Two: *Exhale through your mouth with a restriction through the back of your throat.*

Open your mouth and exhale with an audible, oceanic tone. Release any blame that's connected to your negative feeling. Take full responsibility for having that feeling.

Step Three: *Repeat the inhale-and-exhale cycle.*

On the inhale, focus on the acceptance of your current negative feeling. On the exhale, release any resistance to that feeling.

Step Four: *Repeat the inhale-and-exhale cycle again.*

This time on the inhale, find where the feeling lives in your physical body and experience the feeling as an energy rather than an emotion. On the exhale, use the breath to activate the energy and visualize it circulating throughout the body.

Step Five: *On the final inhale, keep your eyes closed and look up to your third eye, the point above and between your eyebrows.*

Draw your breath all the way up to your head. Simultaneously hold your gaze at your third-eye point and your breath for 30 seconds. Feel yourself as the unattached witness to your experience.

Step Six: *For the final exhale, release with an audible sound.*

On this release, make a powerful "O" sound for the duration of your exhale, as long and slow as possible. Feel yourself releasing the energy by moving it out of your body in synchronicity with your breath. Anchor yourself into the present moment and notice the peacefulness and choicelessness that occurs.

Practice Presence over Comparison

I'm not so naive to say that all our problems begin and end with love. Life can be hard—and we certainly know that love and fear aren't the only things that polarize our beliefs, thoughts, behaviors, and feelings.

The past and the future are both constantly vying for our attention, pulling at us like the North and South Poles and jockeying for a significant role in our systems.

Whether at work or at home, we make reference points out of our memories of the extreme highs and lows of our past. And we are all drawn to the seductive possibility of the future.

But when we give in to the magnetic pull of either, we suspend ourselves in a constant, counterproductive state of comparison. The problem with living in a state of comparison is that all we're really creating is a "phantom present"—a rather diluted version where you don't really have to commit to doing anything now because you're too busy talking about how it was or how it will be.

Think for a moment about how a lot of us talk about the past, or when someone refers to a time when the pace might have been slower—when our smartphones didn't keep us on call at all times, when we weren't tethered mentally and physically to our jobs at all hours of the day. We hear things like "Life was better back then. Life was easier then."

In some ways, sure, that might be true . . . but let's look at the workplace as an example. While organizational memory is valuable for many reasons, when not fostered and used properly, it can embolden us to romanticize suboptimal systems of the past and abandon accountability today. Because let me assure you, the past was not always better—which is probably why Dr. Hawkins often encouraged us to let it go.

Take the weekend, for instance—it's actually a relatively new introduction to the American workspace. Until 1922, Ford Motor Company employees worked six days a week. It took Edsel Ford, Henry Ford's son and the president of the company at the time, to admit that people need more than one day a week for rest or recreation.[15]

Wider adoption of the 48-hour weekend didn't come until the 1930s. And even then, it wasn't entirely for the mental and physical benefit of the worker. In fact, as Americans became more interested in the Saturday "Football Craze," more and more brands and entertainment venues began looking at it as a new profit opportunity for growing the leisure industry.[16]

Today, could you imagine not having a weekend?

Really, think about that: This was a time when the concept of burnout, or a concern for mental health, weren't just taboo. They weren't even things people considered or knew about at all, which meant there were no policies and protections in place. We still have a long way to go in terms of the intersection of capitalism and compassion for the human condition, but we're certainly better off today in that at least these are topics gaining attention.

When you look at a company's history, you can see it's never a straight line. There are setbacks and successes. And the same goes for ourselves.

The stories of what has transpired leading up to this exact moment in our lives—they stay with us. They are woven into the fabric of our identity—personal, business, or otherwise. Which means that whether or not we want them to, our experiences can tether us to a past that no longer serves our well-being or a future that may never come.

But because they are such a big part of our identities, when we try to focus on the transformational power of the present, we can also feel the pain of letting another part of us go. And often, that not only looms largely on how we handle the present, but it reawakens within us a crisis at the core of the human condition: the crisis of comparison.

We look at our peers, our friends, and our relatives, and then we create narratives about our own timeline of success based on theirs. We compulsively check the pedometer on our smartphones, count calories, and monitor our sleep and meditation times, turning even our best efforts at calming our bodies and minds into sources of comparison.

We are defining the breadth of ourselves with a behavioral pattern that requires us to simultaneously undermine it. And the result of this comparative language? A codified, toxic formula for othering those around us and for displacing us from the most important and intentional piece of the puzzle: the now.

We are, after all, coded and programmed to believe, "There's always tomorrow."

But the antidote is clear. Practicing presence over comparison—yet another one of our key intentions—is a path we can all connect with in our own way.

Following my divorce, I had this overwhelming feeling that everything I'd worked so hard for had been taken away from me. I had had a beautiful wife and picture-perfect marriage, social status, and a burgeoning business empire. When it all started to crumble at once, it felt like everything I had been lauded for, everything people had celebrated about my life and my achievements, was suddenly gone. But it wasn't the collapse of the relationships or the business that was at the core of my shame. It was the feeling of failure in comparison to the people around me.

It wasn't until years later that I completely accepted the power of the present moment and stopped to realize that all of it was a beautiful opportunity to look at what I did have. My ego crumbled, and I had a profound sense of awareness. Even though I had less in financial resources than I had expected by that point, I still had complete freedom over my life and was able to take time off, which was a blessing. Three things surfaced for me during this time that aligned me with what I consider to be the highest states of being.

Love. I felt the love of family. My now-partner and I had made the commitment of going on a spiritual journey together to bring more love into our lives and had begun preparing to conceive our first child.

Peace. I felt the peace of having a home. Previously, home was never something that landed with me. My physical home was a source of great anxiety, and my efforts to create a place where I could feel safe and loved over the years always had some derivative pain attached to them. It felt like I was either running from what I hadn't dealt with in Australia or I was trying to make a new home based on the idea that I would create the opposite of everything I'd had as a child. When I came to Aspen, it was different. I claimed it as my home, and that decision felt natural and nurturing.

Joy. I felt the joy in doing my life's work and knowing that work was meaningful. The work I had done with the Intentionality methodology and frameworks had ignited so many different creative opportunities and collaborations, and being able to witness the thousands of people transformed by its message had become very meaningful to me.

Rooting myself in the present allowed me to wake up—and when I did, I stopped comparing who I was to whom I was on the path to become.

One thing about presence that is incredibly important to note is that if it were easy, if it were on autopilot from the get-go, then we wouldn't need Intentionality. Practicing presence inevitably involves setbacks—setbacks that must be treated as an undeniable part of any evolution. So if you take two steps forward and one step back, don't give up. Just remember that presence is and will always be within your reach.

I once worked with a founder whose company had a huge setback and who struggled a great deal with eliminating comparison from both his vocabulary and his vision for the brand. The company was suffering a drastic decrease in profits, and as such, the founder's personal net worth took a significant hit. While he was still better off than most, he felt a great deal of shame about the financial loss.

This founder seemed to be struggling with some of the very same ego and identity challenges I had as an entrepreneur, and I didn't hesitate to share my story. By identifying that there were common denominators in our challenges, and by sharing my path, I was able to prevent patterns of commiseration and comparison and instead create a safe space for us to navigate the present.

In his negative belief loop, he was comparing himself to where he was and where he thought he should be at this point in his life. His thoughts were harsh: *What an idiot I am. If only I had what I had before. I can't believe I messed this up.*

And it wasn't long before we discovered that his core negative belief was "I am not enough."

Negative Belief Loop

I asked the founder how he wanted to feel. He wanted what most of us want: acceptance—especially self-acceptance. He wanted confidence and sincerity in his life and his relationships.

Of course he understood this likely wouldn't happen overnight. At first, the desires of his logical, conscious mind weren't syncing up with his subconscious programming. A lifetime of measuring self-worth by comparing himself to his high-performing peers and messages from the media was making it hard for him to convince himself that he was worthy despite the financial loss. So I suggested that I guide him through a process called Emotional Clearing (you'll learn more about this in Chapter 7).

The process brought him back to kindergarten and a memory of his teacher holding his drawing of a dog up next to one of his classmate's and asking the class which project was done the correct way. My client had colored his dog purple, and the teacher favored the student who'd drawn the more traditional dog with brown fur. The humiliation of being outed in front of his entire class for not doing the assignment "correctly" had stuck with him, quite literally in his system, for his entire life.

By the end of our 60-minute session, he had released this energy and generated compassion for his younger self. We then created a positive belief loop and came up with behaviors he knew he could commit to. These included a daily practice of gratitude journaling and 15 minutes of meditation. His new, positive belief loop started with "I am enough," and his mind began to generate new, positive thoughts like, *This is exactly where I need to be.* He was finally able to practice presence over comparison—and he could, at last, feel how he wanted to feel.

Positive Belief Loop

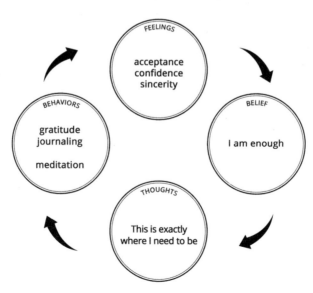

FEELINGS

acceptance
confidence
sincerity

BELIEF

I am enough

BEHAVIORS

gratitude
journaling

meditation

THOUGHTS

This is exactly
where I need to be

There is power in presence, and that's what I was able to help my client experience firsthand that day. Whether within an organization or within yourself, being present will allow you to transform your relationship with your past—and perhaps that's why it's referred to as the present: because it's truly a gift.

Try giving yourself that gift right now with this next circuit breaker.

Circuit Breaker:
The Concentration Breath

In this exercise, you'll focus on your breath and sensations to help you truly abandon the allure of the past or the present and opt instead to feel the energy and possibility of the moment. Note that your concentration is the key to continuing with the concurrent movements. At any point in time, if you become too attuned to one of them, bring yourself back to all three. Conveniently, this exercise can be done almost anywhere. You could be doing this in the midst of a conversation or in a loud place with sensory overload and use it to get yourself into an observational and nonjudgmental state.

Step One: *Start observing your breath—in and out through your nose.*

As you breathe in and out of your nose, match the length of your exhale to that of your inhale in a nice, circular breathing cycle. Feel the air coming in and out of your nostrils.

Step Two: *Begin rubbing your tongue on the roof of your mouth very softly and gently.*

Make sure you continue paying attention to your breath. And now begin to notice your tongue connecting to the roof of your mouth. Notice the textures and sensations.

Step Three: *Rub your thumb and index fingers together on both hands very slowly, softly, and with small movements.*

While still watching your breath and moving the tongue on the roof of your mouth, start rubbing your fingers together. Notice the pressure on the thumb pads of both hands while concurrently observing the sensations you're igniting in all three areas of your body at once.

Prioritize Feelings over Outcomes

When I was elected president of the Entrepreneurs' Organization Colorado chapter, the theme I proposed for the year was "Be Intentional"—and I did my best to embody that concept. I had a grand vision for what we could achieve over the year and the lasting impact we could have on the chapter. We were on track for every metric outlined in the year's vision and were even ahead of schedule in many regards.

I was about 10 months into my term, and everything was going great. Then the pandemic hit.

The world came to a grinding halt, and in an instant, it became clear that everything I'd outlined and everything the board had envisioned for the year and worked so hard for would also be halted. I wrestled with that disappointment, and my ego came out to play. I started spinning and worrying that I personally wasn't going to be remembered as a great chapter president who made a lasting impact.

For hours this energy built up in my system. My negative belief loops were activated, and I was all over the place. Thankfully, I remembered to use a circuit breaker. When I was in army officer training in Australia, whenever we were dropped into combat, the first thing we had to do was slow down our breathing so we didn't panic and miss important directives. A flash of that coding washed over me, inspiring me to take a breath. Because this experience of being in a pandemic was new to me—and to all of us—I felt limited in what I could do intellectually. I knew that what I really needed to do was to drop into my heart, the easiest way to access my intuition and ground myself.

As I did this, an insight came to me. My theme for the year was "Be Intentional." And if that's what I truly meant, then surely I must have prepared myself in some way for a situation like this? Perhaps not precisely a pandemic, but surely I had a strategy for overcoming an obstacle that presented itself, right?

So I revisited the vision document that I'd created with the board for the year. When I reflected on the things I knew we now weren't going to be able to do together, I felt sad and disappointed. For a moment, I felt worse than before I'd looked at it. But then I reread the document and saw something that trumped everything else on the page. It was my own handwritten note that said, "Intention for the Year: To Be Proud of Our Leadership."

Taking pride in leadership is not a finite aspiration. The revelation I had was that intention was still very much on the table and unconstrained by our metrics or the circumstances that were preventing us from gathering in person. That pridefulness was a feeling. It was a bolt of lightning reminding me that we were alive, we were fortunate to be here, and we had the ability to adapt.

I asked myself what I would need to do in the moment so that I could look back and say I was proud of our leadership. This question helped release the stronghold my ego had on me and gave me the permission and inspiration to spring into action.

I organized the first virtual town hall in the chapter to reinstill confidence in everyone and to show that they weren't alone during this crisis, that we would always be there for anything our members needed help with. We also kicked off a scholarship fund. We mobilized our resources, and much of the work we did was replicated by chapters around the world.

For me, this was a game-changing example of learning what's possible when we prioritize our feelings over outcomes. The metrics changed for that year. When we came together, which was now all virtually, it took on a new level of personal significance, humanity, and connectedness. I know that if the challenge had never arisen, we would not have felt the closeness or the pride we felt in troubleshooting, and eventually transforming, our chapter. And the pride we felt in perseverance was very different and much more profound than if we weren't faced with the challenge of leading through a crisis.

This is not to say that you should throw outcomes or goals out the window entirely. But it does mean that if you flip the order of your priorities, it will make all the difference in the world. It's still a very real necessity to have things you aspire to or reach for—but your outcomes and goals should be focused on supporting your desired feelings.

Prioritizing our feelings over outcomes provides flexibility. It enables us to win even if we lose. It empowers us to use our inner feelings to drive the ever-changing outer world in a more positive way.

And that's why, for me, out of all of the key intentions at the core of Intentionality, this is the master key. Intentionality is a feelings-first approach to living and leadership—which means that prioritizing feelings over outcomes can always be the cornerstone you return to when in doubt or veering off your path. It's a way to put yourself back in the driver's seat and take control of reimagining and recoding your way forward.

The world has programmed us to always look ahead, to focus on the outcomes above all else. Traditionally speaking, the world operates on prioritizing the endgame. Everything we do in our personal and professional lives is colored by this mindset. Consider how we design our org charts, our workflows, and our goals. It's often driven by statements like "It's how you finish that counts," or "Keep your eyes on the prize." With society putting feelings in second position to outcomes, we have learned to accept and reinforce an outdated negative belief loop—one that in the case of business often results in a staggeringly negative bottom line.

My rock bottom had been a double whammy because I had been partners with Sarah in business and in life. While I was struggling with the collapse of my business and my marriage, I realized that this concept of incentivizing everyone by advising them to focus solely on the outcome wasn't going to cut it. I was spinning, and my negative belief loops were out in full force. So I started focusing on what was next, and on what step I could take to get me to the next chapter in my life. But there was just one problem: I hadn't given myself the space to *feel* first.

At that time, I reflected a great deal on Dr. Hawkins's belief that to let go of the past, you have to let go of thinking. His explanation of what's happening and what's at stake when we overthink is truly profound. He said that our minds tell us we have to think and plan in order to survive. It's certainly what I was wired to do. It's what we all do on autopilot at one point or another. But what this really means, word for word according to him, is that to let go of thinking, "You really have to, in a way, give up the will to survive."[17]

Now when you first hear that, it may seem harsh. It may seem pessimistic. But give it a moment of reflection. This sentence, in many ways, saved my life.

The simultaneous ending of my marriage and business, and more importantly the life Sarah and I had thought we were building together, became so difficult for me because I was in a constant battle with my coding that pushed me to think, to plan, and to focus on the future. It kept telling me, "Just focus on what's next, and this will all be behind you. The sooner you have a plan and move on, the sooner you'll find new success in love and work." But all of that *felt*—in my soul—awful. It felt like I was off my axis and that something was missing.

Remember my core negative belief loop?

Negative Belief Loop

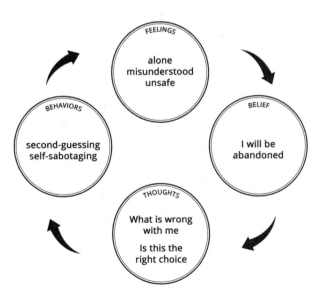

My primary conflict with my coding was rooted in an extraordinary fear of abandonment, which meant that my body and mind were almost always functioning in survival mode. I was sending signals to myself without even knowing it, telling myself that merely avoiding abandonment was an acceptable, if not ideal, outcome.

But I woke up one day and realized that none of it was working. That's when I said, "I don't ever want to feel like this again." Notice, I didn't say, "I don't ever want to *think* this way again." I said, "I don't ever want to *feel* this way again."

This is when I had an epiphany. Survival mode felt like shit because it never actually involved me feeling in real time. It was just a way for me to think my way out of a challenge that demanded much more of my emotions than I was willing to allow.

So I said to myself, *What can I let go of? What deliberate path can I take from here on out so that my body and mind never go through this battle again?*

The first draft of my first positive belief loop was just a list—a simple list of 16 things I knew had the potential to make me feel better and stronger each day. This was my permission slip to feel my way back to wholeness and to savor the steps along the way.

And for the first time, I believed I could change. I didn't need to wait for something to happen **to** me. I didn't need to wait for someone to do something **for** me. I could be the architect of my own transformation, as long as I believed that what's next is **now**.

Because the truth is that negative belief loops put you in no-man's-land. You're neither in the past, present, nor future. You're hovering unproductively between the three at all times—never spending enough time in one spot to make any substantial progress in feeling how you desire to feel.

On the other hand, positive belief loops firmly root you in the present. They empower you to reclaim feeling as an asset. The past will always feel far—and the future will always feel out of reach. But the present is the place you can actually feel and act on *right now*.

After I realized that no one except me is in charge of my happiness, I was able to prioritize my feelings instead of getting lost in the hopes of a better future.

And what really helped me to jump-start my system was utilizing the power of breath. I've found that it is the easiest and most efficient way to train your mind and body to override its negative loops. Breath will always be your most tactile resource for rejecting the toxic behavior of outcome-driven living, and for ensuring that the feelings you desire become your driving force.

The Breath of Joy is one circuit breaker that's specifically designed to help you reprioritize and begin that transformation. *And* it's a lot of fun!

Circuit Breaker:
The Breath of Joy

This breath is guaranteed to put you into a state of joy, just as its name implies. There are other benefits as well—such as increasing oxygen levels in your bloodstream, moving energy through your body, and releasing stress.

You'll be doing this breath standing and will need some space—a good rule of thumb is to put your arms out to your sides and spin in a circle before you start, making sure you don't hit anything.

Step One: *Stand upright and gently close your lips, placing a gentle smile on your face.*

Your feet should be shoulder-width apart and parallel, knees slightly bent, and arms dangling by your side.

Step Two: *Inhale one-third of your air through your nose and raise your arms in front of you.*

Arms should be parallel to each other at shoulder level with your palms facing up.

Step Three: *Inhale another one-third of your air through your nose and raise your arms out to your sides.*

Arms should open like wings at shoulder level into a T formation.

Step Four: *Inhale the final third of your air through your nose, sweeping your arms in front of you and then raising them overhead.*

As you are approaching nearly full lung capacity with this final inhale, your arms are parallel, palms are facing each other, and fingertips are reaching toward the ceiling.

Step Five: *Swing your arms toward the ground as you bend at the waist and let out all your air through your mouth with an audible "ha" sound.*

Let the momentum of your arms draw you toward the ground as you bend your knees into a squat position and let your arms sweep behind you. Your head and neck will dangle for a short pause before you begin the next round.

Step Six: *Repeat Steps Two through Five 10 more times.*

After you finish 11 rounds of the Breath of Joy, allow yourself to hang toward the ground on the final exhale for a few extra seconds, letting gravity pull everything down. Slowly return to standing, close your eyes, and let your arms dangle by your sides. Keep the gentle smile on your face as you relax into your body. Notice the flow of energy you have activated. You might feel a tingling sensation in your fingertips or palms of your hands and the increased beating of your heart. This is a quick way to generate joy, a high-vibrational state that will be magnetic to others and connect you with your desired feelings.

KEY TAKEAWAYS

Leverage Energy over Time

- Time is the standard metric for how we prioritize what is important to us, but when we shift our focus to energy, we become more aware, more present, and are less likely to get lost in negative belief loops.

- Look at your calendar. Is there a meeting, appointment, or commitment that defaults to a certain amount of time that you could shorten? Edit at least one of these events in the next week, and then schedule in a 10- or 20-minute self-care break with the time saved.

Embrace Discipline over Rigidity

- Rigidity frames things from a punitive lens, while discipline, when implemented with compassion, is an act of self-love.

- Challenge yourself to squeeze in some form of exercise this week in a time slot that you typically would have written off as wasted time. It could be going for a 15-minute walk, doing 50 push-ups, or dropping into a 1-minute plank.

Choose Love over Fear

- Every human being has the potential for change, and when the world offers infinite avenues for a fear-driven existence, choosing love is the ultimate path forward.

- Think of a recent event or encounter that resulted in you having a negative reaction. See if you can get to the root of what triggered you—not the act itself, but what it activated within you. This will be a core emotion like feeling unworthy, unseen, unlovable, unvalued, inadequate, insignificant, helpless, or rejected. Replace that feeling with love by walking it through the four steps of Emotional Clearing:

1. Become aware of the feeling

2. Accept the feeling

3. Experience the feeling as an energy rather than an emotion

4. Witness the experience as a passive observer

Practice Presence over Comparison

- The past and the future are both constantly vying for our attention, but rooting yourself in the present moment is where you can let go of comparison and wake up to your true nature.

- Try doing the Concentration Breath the next time you are at a social event or in a meeting and see how easily you can covertly do this circuit breaker to bring you back to the present moment.

Prioritize Feelings over Outcomes

- It's important to have things you aspire to or reach for—but your outcomes and goals should be focused on supporting your desired feelings as this ensures long-lasting satisfaction and fulfillment.

- Think of the last time you had a big disappointment or setback. Identify what your expectations were and how you were let down. Now identify what desired feelings you could have focused on instead of only measuring success on the intended outcome. Would those feelings have driven different behaviors on your part, or perhaps a different response to the outcome?

CHAPTER 7

ENERGY
INTERVENTIONS

Repetition may be the primary driving force for your recoding, but sometimes you'll need what I refer to as an *energy intervention* to jump-start your path to Intentionality.

So, what is an energy intervention? How do you know when you need it? And how can it help you recode?

As we discussed, coding and recoding happens through repetition of belief loops, which means that the greater number and the stronger the impressions we have of them, the more dominant role they will play in our subconscious. But it also means they are accessible for override.

In a perfect world, where you are free of all prior negative impressions, you probably wouldn't have to worry about the need for energy interventions. But no one lives in that world, because it doesn't exist. And the reason that world doesn't exist is that our environment is filled with external influencers and various people, perspectives, and factors that play a role in forming our thoughts, shaping how we choose to behave and ultimately how we feel.

On any given day, regardless of how well your positive belief loop creation may be going, you could be jolted back into traumatic circumstances, reminders of a difficult time in your past, or even confronted with challenges you thought you'd overcome but are still lingering dormant in your system. You start falling back into your old ways. You resort back to those old belief loops that feel comfortable, even if they never served you. And you unintentionally counteract all the progress you've made.

At this fork in the road, you may feel that you have enough information, resources, and tools to return to recoding through repetition. On the other hand, you may need something out of the ordinary, something more extreme that stops the hamster wheel, kicks you into gear, and instantly reconnects you with your desired feelings. You need something that can help you swiftly clear old imprints and find your way back to your path.

Enter the energy intervention. Think of it like the process of cleaning your teeth. Repetition is the behavior-based approach to keeping them clean—every day you brush and floss your teeth. You repeat this daily habit of dental hygiene just as you would repeat behaviors to press upon and imprint your positive belief loops every day. But even if you brush your teeth and floss regularly, at some point, you'll need a deep dental clean. You'll need an intervention with perhaps reconstructive work to get your mouth into shape and rid it of any plaque, cavities, or possible infections.

Energy interventions interrupt our deep-rooted coding and are what I've found to be analogous to an incredibly powerful deep clean at the dentist. There are a great number of energy interventions. Here are a few that I've used personally and are some of my favorites for accessing a higher level of consciousness.

Breathwork

Throughout this book, you've learned circuit breakers, the breath exercises designed not only to help you prevent the formation of new negative belief loops, but to act as a pattern interrupt when an old loop is activated. Another type of breathwork I'd like to introduce here is one that functions not as a deterrent but as an energy intervention. This breath uses an intense amount of energy combined with subconscious priming, breath holds, and visualizations that allow you to effectively "clean out" your system. When you go into the theta state during this intervention, you can use the data you garner to imprint new positive belief loops. In other words, this energy intervention is specifically used for a release and a recode.

A few years ago, while visiting one of my favorite surf beaches in Panama, I was asked to lead a breath journey in collaboration with a DJ friend of mine. The group gathered on a wooden deck on the beach at sunset, and soon the space was full. This specific destination attracts people from all over the world, so because of this eclectic mix and the full moon rising overhead, an intense energy was building.

When I'm guiding these sessions, I'm not in my thinking mind. I'm a servant to the divine feminine, the nurturing energy that isn't focused on *doing* but rather on *being*. It is a meditative experience for me even though I'm exuding a ton of energy. I connect on an energetic level with the group, and I allow my intuition to guide me where I need to go—which on this particular evening was toward a young woman in the group. I felt an undeniable pull to her and sensed a strong field of energy around her stomach and womb region. I could see there was a resistance happening. I often see this in facial expressions and body tension—but in this case, there was also an energetic heaviness in the field around her, something that was telling me she was ready for a release and recode.

I started sending love and light to her, and as I cued the guided breath hold, with her permission, I placed my hands gently on her stomach to let her know that I was there and that she was supported. I could feel her start shaking, and at the end of the breath hold, as she let out a big exhale, her whole body relaxed. Her partner was next to her, and I could sense his connection with her experience. I gently placed their hands together as they lay in the peace and stillness of that moment. We moved on to where I was being energetically called on other parts of the deck and completed the ceremony as the full moon synchronistically emerged from behind the clouds.

The next day the couple asked me, "How did you know to connect with us at that exact moment?" I shared my experience of feeling the intuitive call, the resistance, and then the transmutation of energy into trust, surrender, and acceptance. They then shared with me that they were on vacation recovering from the trauma of a late-stage miscarriage. They'd needed to get away because everything at home was a reminder of their loss. And then the woman shared that during the breath journey, she had met her baby and had come to peace with the limited amount of time they had shared in this lifetime. She said that she felt a physical and emotional shift into a new state of acceptance and was ready to let her partner back in; you could see the visible relief and restoration in his eyes, and it was a beautiful thing to witness.

I'll never forget this woman and her husband because they were so open to the experience, so graceful with themselves and so grateful for the ability to return home and move forward with a renewed sense of peace. I'm constantly in a state of awe for the role I get to play in people's cathartic experiences with breath and the stories they share in the aftermath. And what is so magical about the breath is that you can create a safe container anytime and anywhere—it is the most low-maintenance of any of the interventions. These more intense practices of breathwork empower you to heal yourself by releasing energies from traumas or past pain by reconnecting you with the Universal Mind and by giving you the opportunity to recode with positive belief loops.

Psychedelics

I have used psychedelics many times in my life, and for me they have proven to be a powerful tool in uprooting what I see as my internal "muck." On one 12-day intensive ayahuasca journey, I was in the lower Andes, in the Amazonian jungle in Tarapoto, Peru. The months leading up to my trip had been particularly stressful and taxing. There was uncertainty around the renewal of my work visa in America, and it clouded every part of my decision-making and life. As soon as I received the long-awaited documents, I tuned in to an overwhelming message that I couldn't ignore—I needed to reset my energy. Despite some initial disappointment, I postponed my party trip to Ibiza and instead rerouted to a spiritual journey in Peru.

When I arrived, I journeyed deep into the jungle, intentionally taking myself out of contact with the rest of the world for what would be a series of seven ayahuasca ceremonies over 12 days. As anyone who has sat with "the grandmother" (a nickname for ayahuasca because the experience mimics a mother's healing with love—and often tough love) will tell you, you are on her schedule. I was committed to this complete and total reboot, but to say I was nervous would be an understatement.

Ayahuasca ceremonies typically begin around 8 P.M. and can go for any length of time, but they usually wrap up in the early hours of the morning. The daytime agenda included yoga sessions, clean eating, rest, and relaxation. During the fourth ceremony, I experienced an incredible energy intervention. Two shamans, a man and a woman, were leading the ceremony—which was excellent because I needed their collective masculine and feminine energies. I let them flow through me and soon enough, I realized this ceremony was about my mother and father.

I dropped into the moment, to the energy and sacred rituals of the ceremony, and I surrendered to the experience. As the female shaman guided me, I started to feel the energy of my mom, and a flood of memories with her over the course of my life surfaced. I felt the cells in my body releasing energy and could sense that the pain I had wasn't really about me. It was just part of my lineage. It wasn't mine to hang on to anymore, and it all flooded out of my body. When the male shaman came, the same thing happened with memories of my father. I felt a rush of energy coming down through my body from top to bottom. I felt a full release of the cords connecting me to my parents. It sounds weird to say, but I felt I had forgiven them on a cellular level, and I felt free.

I'll always hold on to this one specific moment. There I was, deep in the Amazonian jungle—and the old coding was coming up. My memories of childhood, and of parents whose actions I never wanted to replicate, were all stirring within me and bursting at the seams. Suddenly this final wave of energy blasted through my big toes and all the way up into my body. It was an intensity I'd felt only one other time in my life, and that was what I refer to as my "awakening" on the Camino de Santiago. I was now experiencing total bliss. Everything made sense, and I heard myself saying out loud, "Holy shit, I'm ready to be a dad."

After coming out of the ceremony and recalibrating with my conscious mind, I woke up the following day with zero doubts about becoming a father. I couldn't wait to reunite with my partner and share the news. I had a level of certainty I'd never known or dreamed I could reach.

Be curious about what might be calling you, as it may be an opportunity for physical and emotional release—one that, like me, you might not even know you need. Surrender to not knowing and fully trusting the process and power of this type of energy intervention. And equally of importance is to be very selective and intentional about how you access and receive it.

Extreme Temperatures

Between Christmas and New Year's Eve in 2021, I traveled to Lake Tahoe with my partner. We were out snowshoeing and she was frustrated, not by the weather or the difficult trek at hand, but because of the difficult emotions she'd been struggling with over the previous few days. She admitted that she was mired in a victim mentality, but nonetheless, she felt like she couldn't control her anger and was stuck spinning in a loop. Finally she blurted out, "I would do anything to not feel this way right now."

She was about to turn back to the house and end our hike early when I turned back to her and asked, *"Anything?"*

There was silence, and then I could see the wheels turning in her head. She knew that if given permission, I would push her to break out of her negative belief loop. She also knew how much I loved a good cold plunge and that we had very easy access. After all, we were in Lake Tahoe. But she didn't say anything, and because she seemed more deflated than I'd seen her in quite some time, I let it go.

We returned home together, and as I was parking the car, she went into the house. To my surprise, she came back out holding two towels and got into the car. She was staring straight ahead, and the only words she uttered were, "Just go before I change my mind."

We went down to the water. It was snowing, and I could feel the energy building as I guided us in some tummo-style breathing, an ancient Tibetan technique designed to raise body temperature using visualization and muscle contractions. She still refused to make eye contact, but she was there and willing—and as we approached the water, I turned her toward me and said, "You can do this. I believe in you."

So we held hands and walked into the freezing water, where we stayed for about two and a half minutes. For the final minute, we locked eyes. The extreme cold of the water sent an electric shock through our bodies and catapulted us forward into a new energetic state. And despite the freezing temperatures, as we exited the water, she had an entirely relaxed persona, both in her speech and her body language.

In a surprising and synchronistic moment, the couple we were staying with happened to be walking by the lake, and they saw the whole thing. They took photos and captured our embrace. In one of the photos, our heads were locked into a perfect heart shape—memorializing a huge moment when my partner didn't succumb to her negative belief loop and instead transcended her state with love. She used a physiological change to change her psychological state.

Other ways to use extreme temperatures as energy interventions are saunas, sweat lodges, or (one of my favorites) the Mesoamerican tradition of *temazcal*. The temazcal ceremony is done in an igloo-like structure typically made from stone, mud, or clay. The environment is created to simulate the womb with hot and humid temperatures (up to 120 degrees Fahrenheit) and pitch-black darkness. You typically sit on the ground for two or more hours as you honor each of the four elements: earth, water, wind, and fire. A shaman leads you through rituals including chanting and the honoring of ancestors, using a variety of instruments like rattles, drums, and shakers, and throwing water and herbs onto the hot stones. This is all designed to yield a range of physiological and psychological responses that empower you to push your limits in both the body and the mind. When you emerge from the temazcal, you are born anew.

These are a few tangible ways for you toovercome resistance, endure discomfort, and override your conditioned mind with a blast to the system.

Sound

A few years ago, I traveled to Sedona with my partner. Sedona is one of these incredible places where when you arrive, you can immediately feel the energy vortex—one that draws you into its core with the promise of healing and changing the equilibrium of your energetic state.

One evening at dinner, we had a disagreement, and she stormed out of the restaurant. And it wasn't the first time we'd been in conflict; she had been having abrupt and explosive outbursts sporadically throughout the day while we were hiking. I felt as though she was out-of-body and unaware of the consequences—that she didn't quite understand how much energy she was casting into the ether and how much destruction was in her wake. In fairness to her, we'd been through a lot of navigating in our newish relationship, and we were both still learning just how interconnected our ability to both hurt and heal each other might be.

But it was during this meal when I started to become concerned about these projections and wondered if exploring and harmonizing our energy fields was going to be sustainable in the long run. I was alone at the table, feeling a bit lost. I'd reached the point where despite wanting to remain in the relationship, I did not know how to show up for it and for her while still honoring my needs. While sitting there in a bit of shock, I saw two young women a couple tables away. They were laughing with the waitress and really engaged with one another, and I couldn't help wishing that I was a part of it. This feeling came over me, and I felt like I needed to know what they were talking about. I don't know why. Sometimes the universe provides little tugs in a direction, and you have to decide if you'll follow the lead.

When the waitress returned, I asked her what the women had been talking about. She told me that they had just had an incredible experience with a local healer who specialized in sound journeys. Sedona is not a big place, and thankfully the healer was well-known, so the waitress happily gave me her number.

By this point it was 8:45 P.M., and in other circumstances I would have waited to call. But I couldn't. Something was pulling me to this woman. I dialed her number, and she answered after the first ring. "You don't know me," I said. "But I just got your number from a waitress, and I have an intuitive insight that I need to see you."

The healer responded, "Well, I could probably fit you in in three days' time."

I didn't pause in my next response; it just flowed out of me. "I don't think you understand. I mean now." With an unprecedented level of conviction, I waited to hear her response.

Within a few seconds, I felt an energetic shift happen between us. She said, "I was just wrapping up for the day, but if you can come now, I'll see you."

I walked out to the car, and my partner was sitting in the front seat, crying. She was distraught. "I found someone who's going to help us, and we're going there now," I told her.

And she looked up at me and replied, "Why are you so wonderful?" It was one of the kindest things she'd ever said, and I needed to hear it.

So we drove to a cabin out in the desert, arriving around 10:00 P.M., and this beautiful, blonde French woman was waiting inside on a big mat. There were flutes and drums, sound bowls and chimes, and almost any other instrument you could imagine. She'd laid two rugs out for both of us. She introduced herself and began to explain the sound journey, the universal laws of vibration, and more specifically that we're all made of frequency and sometimes get out of alignment.

We both lay down and started relaxing, and as we listened to an arc of different sounds, we drifted into a different realm. At one point, I had a vision of another person lying on their back, breathing in and out through the mouth to a distinct rhythm. And then I received a message that said, "Do this breath. It's not only going to help you and your partner—it's going to impact the world." I looked over, and my partner was so peaceful. I was peaceful. And while I'd never really had a premonition like this before, something about it put me at ease. I felt so free of the heaviness my partner and I had entered the experience with. We were able to come back together because we used the sound journey and its particular vibrational frequencies to find our equilibrium, and to find our way back into energetic alignment.

A few days later, I found myself thinking about the vision I had and wondered what its message might mean. So I tried doing the breath on my own, intuitively following what I'd tapped into in that sound journey, and it was transformational—unlike anything else I'd ever experienced. Shortly after, I was asked to lead a session in my camp's "soul series" at Burning Man. I'd become so connected to this breath and had an innate confidence that I could lead others in experiencing it.

Everything about it was intuitive—the music selections, the breathing patterns and holds, what I was saying, what I was doing, and the channeling of energy. I was in awe of what was coming through me—because it was no longer just a breath. It was an energy coursing through me and out to the 100 or more people in attendance. Since then, people have regularly requested to repeat the journey, and I've led tens of thousands of people around the world.

I've been asked how I learned to do it, and I always share that it was something that came to me from a higher source. I tell them about my experience in Sedona, and I tell them about how since our first sound journey, my partner and I regularly use binaural beats with certain frequencies to put us in more meditative, receiving states with each other. I told them about how we've literally learned to fine-tune ourselves into a more loving place.

There are many options available to you for energy interventions with sound at their core. Choose one that feels natural and comforting to you, and always remember something that the healer and my first sound journey taught me: it might be tempting to look for validation in other people, but tap into the gifts you already have within.

Emotional Clearing

On another trip to Sedona, I stopped at my favorite breakfast place to grab a quick bite. It's a quaint roadside spot with a couple of seats, the best healthy waffles on the planet, wellness products, and a shabby little shelf with secondhand books. There were some books stacked up, and this drew my attention because they were some of my favorites—*A New Earth*, *The Four Agreements*, and *The Untethered Soul*. But the fourth one I'd never seen. It had been dogeared throughout and was full of highlights, page marks, and notes. I started skimming through, and it really spoke to me. It was another sign from the universe to follow this next step on my path.

The book was *Emotional Clearing* by John Ruskan (he has since released an updated edition called *Deep Clearing*). I looked up his website and learned about his online program to become a certified facilitator of the process. So that's exactly what I did. My partner and I both did the course and we've incorporated this modality into countless facets of both our personal and professional lives.

Emotional clearing is a deep relaxation process that connects you with your subconscious to release stagnant negative energies that have been stored there. It's a passive state where emotions flow through, with no thoughts or intentions of changing them. There are three key factors in this type of somatic healing that differentiate it from traditional psychotherapy or psychoanalysis. The subject is to:

- remain present with an unpleasant negative emotion
- experience a negative emotion rather than express it
- invoke a positive experience of a negative emotion

During the process, you start with a meditation to slow your brain waves down into an alpha state. Deeply relaxed yet focused, you then follow a guided process to bring emotions up from the subconscious and into conscious awareness. Once you've identified a negative feeling to work with, you'll follow the four steps of the Emotional Clearing process: awareness, acceptance, direct experience, and witnessing.

Sometimes a clearing can be achieved in just one session, and sometimes, if your core belief comes from a variety of different past wounds, it can require a more substantial commitment. The good news is that once you've released the feeling from your system, the correlating negative belief loop loses its power and you now have fertile ground for recoding.

Vision Quest

A vision quest is typically done on your own and is a rite of passage where you intentionally endure a certain set of constraints. This can include things like limited or no access to food and water, remaining in one physical place for the entirety of the quest, and removing distractions apart from what appears in the natural world (e.g., reading, writing, etc.). This is a tradition born of the Native Americans that requires you to stay in a certain spot for four days and four nights with the intent of establishing contact with the spirit world and serves as an opportunity for internal transformation and renewal. The way I've interpreted the concept of the vision quest is doing something in nature where you spend intentional time with yourself in order to connect with the energy of the natural world, which, in itself, is an incredible healing mechanism.

For my birthday every year, I do a pilgrimage that usually entails a physical endurance activity. A few years ago, because of my broken collarbone, that kind of trek was off the table. Instead, I decided to do a vision quest on the land of the StarHouse in the foothills of Boulder, Colorado, where I spent my time in a sacred structure called the Dodecahedron—a geometric figure with 12 pentagonal faces.[1] Because of my limited mobility, I really had to surrender to the physical inconveniences, to be present with my feelings, and to accept the necessity of taking one moment at a time.

It was the end of November, and it was unusually warm for that time of year in Colorado. But on the last day of my quest, which happened to be the morning of my birthday, I woke up to a banging on the roof. The structure is small and built into the ground, so every noise is amplified. We'd had several feet of snow overnight, and the glass roof of the structure was covered. I ventured outside, where it was completely still and quiet, and I walked for a bit, taking in the peacefulness. The moment felt exactly how I pictured Narnia would—the mythical place from C. S. Lewis's book *The Lion, the Witch and the Wardrobe*, which I'd loved as a child. I even recalled how he described in the book that while there was a lot of snow, there wasn't one bit of sound.

Suddenly, a silky, black fox appeared in front of me. It looked me in the eyes, and we had a moment of deep connection. Historically this day had always conjured up unpleasant memories from the 10th-birthday debacle with my father, but this time it was different. I'd undergone a rebirth—coming out of the womb, coming forth from this sacred vessel, and back into the physical world.

This vision quest was a rebirth for my body as well, and specifically for healing my collarbone. I also saw a vision for the role I was going to play in my healing work for others. I saw how I could help raise the collective consciousness by working with top leaders in the world. And it's no coincidence that today, that's what I'm doing.

The simplest way to describe a vision quest is as a journey of sorts, an exploration where you sit with your feelings and allow visions to come to you. You don't search for anything, but you allow the spirit to come through. My advice for deliberating on a vision quest that's right for you is to consider the constraints you want to employ and what your intention is. Ask yourself what boundaries you're willing to endure for the benefit of expanding your consciousness. What aspects of nature inspire you, and what aspects might intimidate you—and are you willing to go there? Ask yourself where you would feel the most grounded or where you could see yourself making the greatest connection with the natural world. Then just do it! The more you think about it, the more reasons you'll find not to do it—so make the commitment and see where your path leads you.

Pilgrimage

After my divorce, I was getting undeniable signs from the universe directing me to the next steps to take on my path. Within a period of two weeks, I had three different signs relating to the Camino de Santiago—a 500-mile pilgrimage across the width of Spain that has been walked for thousands of years. Now this was something I'd always said I wanted to do, but when I saw it mentioned in a magazine article, and then a movie called *The Way* popped up on my what-to-watch list, and then shortly after that, a random person talked to me about their Camino experience, I knew I had to do it. So in the fall of 2017, my brother Tristan and I set out on this great adventure.

Pilgrimages often result when people go in search of something—significance, spirituality, transcendence—whatever the reason, you are drawn there when you are ready. Not only was I curious about the incredible physical challenge we were embarking on, but I thought it would be an unprecedented opportunity for soul-searching. It can be comforting knowing that many others have consecrated the land before you; millions of pilgrims have walked the same path, and you can feel their energy in your footsteps.

Still very raw from my divorce, this trek helped me connect to a purpose bigger than myself, to untether me from the inner turmoil of my relationship, and to open up parts of myself I'd lost touch with. On the Camino there are many other people walking along with you, and it seemed as if the right ones showed up at the exact right time—when I most needed it. These were people of many different ages and cultures and backgrounds, offering me perspectives and consolations I had never considered for myself.

When I set out on the Camino with my brother, I was in the thick of the tremendous pressure one feels after loss: the loss of a loved one, a relationship, a business endeavor, or anything that feels as though it leaves a gaping hole in your existence. I hoped that by immersing myself in nature, with fellow pilgrims, and in the physical intensity, I would somehow magically heal the past—that once I reached the end of the Camino, it would cauterize much of what was still weighing heavy on my head and heart.

But not long after we started the marathon task, I realized that the walk was where the wisdom was. The Camino was where I became a responsible time traveler of sorts, finally able to revisit my past without getting stuck in it. It was where I first truly forgave my father, and more importantly, where I forgave myself. It was where I returned to my truest nature. And I realized that while I set out seeking healing, what I ended up finding was wholeness.

There is a time and a place for healing. But a pilgrimage is something else altogether. It's where you'll endeavor to find the wisdom in your wounds. It's where you will learn—like I did—that there's simple sacredness to be found in the act of walking that far exceeds the striving we do in our everyday lives. And what I will tell you is that a pilgrimage will feel like you're going home—not physically to a place, but like you're coming full circle back to yourself, to your truest nature, and to the exciting possibility of where the next step will lead you.

Sensory Deprivation

Sensory deprivation entails anything that strips one or more of your senses of stimulation. Wearing an eye mask or noise-canceling headphones is an easy way to do this, and then there are things like using a float tank or having a zero-gravity experience. Some of the more advanced meditative practices I've participated in and that would fall into the realm of energy interventions are a Vipassana retreat and a darkness retreat. To clarify, in this context, *advanced* doesn't mean "superior." It just refers to an activity that requires a certain level of dedication and discipline and isn't something you just stumble into casually.

Vipassana is a 10-day course in silent meditation offered in locations all around the world. The practice is one of observance, presence, and impermanence. The courses are completely free; they're sponsored by past participants who wish to pay the experience forward. It's an incredible model that has been offered since 1969. Each day you sit in meditation for about 10 hours, accumulating over 100 hours throughout the retreat. Between your meditations, there's the opportunity for small walks around the property or naps, but the idea is to really sit with yourself and not distract from whatever you're experiencing, be it unpleasant or pleasant. In addition to not speaking, you are not supposed to make eye contact or engage with anyone besides the teachers or servers.

For me, not speaking or interacting with others was easy. The other constraints—no reading, writing, or eating outside of designated mealtimes (of which there are only two: breakfast and lunch) were more challenging. It was hard to wrap my head around how even things that we consider mindful practices, like journaling or reading, can be methods of avoiding our feelings and can be considered addictions. Satya Narayan Goenka, the legendary teacher and founder of the contemporary Vipassana movement, reiterates this message throughout the course via audio and video recordings: "Vipassana is the art of living. Not the art of escaping."

But the real challenge for me surfaced after the end of the 10 days. Two weeks after leaving the peacefulness and tranquility of this very intentional environment, feeling the most grounded and inspired that I had in a long while, my partner's mother died suddenly in a tragic accident. As death (and surely sudden death) does for so many, her passing activated many of my biggest fears and doubts. I was consumed with feelings of loss and sorrow. I was worried about my partner—and bizarrely, this was my second experience with a parent-in-law falling down a set of stairs, resulting in death. I felt a strong sense of déjà vu and my negative core belief loop of abandonment both surfacing. I observed the all-too-familiar feelings surrounding tragedy. But this time,

I remembered what Vipassana had taught me about life: live, don't escape.

I leaned in to my sensations instead of repressing or avoiding them. I became the witness. I did not let my ego trap me into a victim mindset. I allowed the discomfort. I paused, took a breath, and looked at the facts. I was not being abandoned in the present moment. Yes, there were similarities to past experiences and memories, but I was safe, I was an adult, and I was capable of being supportive to my partner, who was going through one of the hardest moments of her life.

I truly believe that my Vipassana course timing was a universal intervention preparing me for this exact moment. The sensory deprivation had allowed me to tune deeper into my inner world, clean out the residue of some lingering negative belief loops, and show up in a time of great distress as a more wholesome being.

KEY TAKEAWAYS

- Energy interventions interrupt our deep-rooted coding and can empower us to heal old wounds and let go of them permanently.

- Energy interventions are like a jump-start to your system and can help you access a higher level of consciousness.

- Pick one of the energy interventions mentioned in this chapter and commit to trying it out. Your local community may have offerings of things like breathwork, sound journeys, or a cold plunge, but you can also access these things using apps, YouTube, or your own cold shower. Get out of your comfort zone, be creative with what's available to you, and be ready for a shift of consciousness!

Part IV

BEHAVIORS AND TOOLS

The future depends on what you do today.

— **MAHATMA GANDHI**

Creating a positive belief loop isn't as easy as snapping your fingers. In addition to the check-ins and circuit breakers designed to help you regulate your energy and stay the course, what is also incredibly powerful is having a clear understanding of what behaviors directly support how you can best love, grow, serve, play, create, and ultimately live your more intentional and expansive life.

We are a culture coded by and consumed with the idea of longevity. But how well do we really understand this obsession? Are we saying we want to live as long as possible, or are we saying we want a better standard of living and quality of life for as long as it is possible to maintain it? Global wellness is a multibillion-dollar industry feeding our fascination but not necessarily answering the most pressing questions and needs within us.

I'm not immune to the allure of turning the clock back. Like anyone else, I think we all wish we could feel young, healthy, and strong for as long as we're here. But let me ask you something. What is the point of spending infinite amounts of money and energy worrying about how long we're going to live and how good we're going to look while doing it, if we aren't using the time we do have to its fullest potential? What are we actually extending?

I'm less concerned with that kind of longevity and more interested with how I can make time *feel* longer. When I go out into nature in a deliberate effort to disconnect from the world for a few days, because of the way I'm living there, it can feel like two weeks. That often gets me thinking, *What if we extrapolated that over half a century?* Consider how many "extra" years of your life you could have. What if a wellness or medical company offered something like this to you? How much would you be willing to pay to have your time back? A lot, I'm sure. But here I am, telling you that's not necessary. I am saying that if we can collapse time and expand our energy with more intentional living, then we can extend our lives and their quality without such hyper commercialization—I believe we can do this with the behaviors and tools already at our disposal.

The behaviors and tools I offer throughout this book will help you discover what to do with all that energy—as well as empower you to perpetually leverage energy over time, embrace discipline over rigidity, choose love over fear, practice presence over comparison, and, at long last, to prioritize feelings over outcomes.

Part IV explores how you can put these five key intentions at the heart of Intentionality into action in your daily life. The behaviors and tools that back up each of the five intentions will not only support you in recoding your mind and realizing your power, but they will guide you through the dynamic experience of feeling and experiencing more of what life has to offer.

It's important to first delineate the difference between behaviors and tools. Behaviors are the overarching ways in which you can regularly recode and live out an intention. Tools are tangible ways to apply the behaviors.

Put more simply, behaviors are acknowledgments of how you want to live with Intentionality. Tools are ways of implementing those behaviors in your daily life.

Let's dive in.

CHAPTER 8

LEVERAGING ENERGY

If leveraging energy over time is the intention we're pursuing, then we can implement the following practical behaviors to meet that challenge. I've found that identifying where I most want to place my energy is a critical part of living with this intention. I often document this in my morning journaling practice to help me be more mindful and accountable to the behaviors that best serve my energy.

Create space to explore these behaviors and see how you might begin introducing them into your daily life. And don't be too hard on yourself. Behaviors for leveraging energy over time don't change a person overnight. Remember, repetition is always the key. These resources will give you a thorough, contextualized tool kit for ensuring that these behaviors—and your recoding—start and stick!

Behaviors

Evaluate What Increases
and Decreases Your Energy

Perform an energy audit.

Ask yourself whether a certain person or situation is giving or taking from your energy. In other words, does a particular person or circumstance add to or take away from how energized you feel during and after an experience with them?

Do more of the activities that add to your energy, and see how you might be able to alter the ones that detract. Sometimes we need to do things we don't love, but oftentimes there is a creative alternative solution.

Own your strengths and play to them.

Nobody is more equipped to identify where you excel than you. You know what comes more naturally to you, what parts of your truest nature can lead to greater equanimity, and how to maximize the skill sets and roles that are your strong suits.

Don't do things that drain your energy.

Drainage is a deal-breaker. Full stop. Delegate and offload as needed, and remember that drainage can also come in the form of a person. You don't need energy vampires in your life or to continue with anything out of habit. Prioritize things that increase your energy and eliminate those that don't.

Learn to Regulate Your Own Energy

Ground yourself.

When you seek to regulate your energy, it's important to have simple ways to physically return to your truest nature. Sleep, nutrition, movement, and exposure to the sun are just a few. If you're at the beach, put your feet in the sand just at the water's edge. Feel the water running up and down and then notice sensations of the sand pulling away. Or try lying on the ground under a tree. Imagine the roots pulling you in and breathing you out. Align your rhythm with that of the world around you.

Change your physiological state.

Using movement and seeking new sensations in your physical body can have a positive effect on your psychological state. Shake your body or get it moving in some way. Social conditioning often tells us that if we aren't sweating or if our heart rate isn't through the roof, then a workout isn't really a workout. But I've learned through life experience that this is a false program. You can choose anything from a light walk to a rigorous hike, or from gentle yoga to a HIIT workout class. Do what appeals most to you, and remember that changing your physiological state doesn't need to be punitive. It's about shifting into a place where you can feel and function at your very best.

Create your own spark.

Your surroundings can make a big difference in how you experience something. Try to bring a heightened sense of awareness to the environments that make you feel the most decisive, creative, and passionate. Find a local café with nice foliage and an artistic vibe, and indulge yourself with a fancy tea and treat. Sit on a porch, feel the breeze, and take in the smell of fresh-cut grass. Even when you're in a dull and unstimulating setting, you can still get creative. I recommend traveling with an altar and energy-clearing kit so you can always create the spark.

Learn to Protect Your Energy

Don't take on energies that aren't yours.

Part of energy regulation is understanding what isn't working. Think of this in terms of a power adapter. When you travel to another country, the power outlets may not automatically align with the plug and device you're carrying with you, and you may need an adapter to ensure your usage is compatible with the new voltage. In life, there are people all around you with conflicting voltages that are simply not compatible with how you'd like to feel. This means that their energy becomes an unnecessary risk for you and can ultimately undermine your effort to optimize your systems and quality of life.

Know your capacity.

First, don't take on too much. One powerful thing you can do to assess your capacity is to examine each commitment you make through a lens as if it were happening now. Ask yourself, *How would I feel about this if it was happening this evening? Would I be excited about going, or would it feel draining to me?* If you don't get a positive feeling or have initial enthusiasm, don't say yes. Second, stop measuring capacity with time. Remember that limits to your capacity can and should be measured by how you want to spend and conserve your energy—which is to say that when you consider additional commitments, find the balance between healthy stimulation and feeling overwhelmed.

Create boundaries and honor them.

When parents take their kids to the bowling alley, they often request "bumpers" or rails so the children can learn the sport but also to bolster the child's self-confidence and to spare them— pun intended—from logging a game with no pins down. This is an example of how parents set boundaries to drive a positive experience for their child. You can and should be doing this for yourself. The word *boundary* often implies the borders that box you into something, but in fact, boundaries can be the most liberating thing you will bring to your life.

Give yourself permission to say no.

And I mean that exactly how I said it. Give yourself the permission to say no without feeling bad or apologizing for it. *No* is a verb—it is an act of empowerment that allows you to explore a new direction and use your energy on something that serves your desired feelings. It can be one of the most intentional and innovative behaviors you bring to your life. I know all too well that when it comes to family and friends, saying no can feel nearly impossible to do. But just remember that within this permission is an opportunity for self-care and nurturing that only you can provide yourself.

Take Charge of Your Day

Practice intentional transitions.

Whether or not you realize it in the moment, you can bring unwanted energy with you from one situation to another. This can unintentionally stir resentment or disappointment in the people who were previously looking forward to seeing you. If you're on a stressful work trip, consider extending the time away for one additional night and allot that time for recharging. That way, you can come home with a much higher energy and appreciation for your friends, family, or partner. Or, if that isn't logistically or financially feasible, come home with a tremendous amount of love. I often come in with a big hug and kiss before even speaking to my partner so that she feels seen and loved. Try this in whatever way will help your loved ones feel that their needs have been met. It can also make reconnection more powerful and alleviate the stress that time apart can have on both of you.

Prioritize your energetic periods.

Schedule your calendar to ensure your highest priorities align with the period of the day where you either have the most energy or when you're capable of charging your battery and tapping into more of that reservoir. If you know you struggle with late afternoons, prioritize what's most important to you during a period earlier in the day, or vice versa. Or book your focused period to follow a scheduled nap or meditation. This self-management technique will leave you feeling more connected and more capable in all areas of your life.

Shorten meetings.

Dialing back the length of time you allot for meetings enables you to create more space for transitions. Our default settings are on the hour and half hour, but that leaves very little breathing room between these commitments. Normalize setting meetings for 20- or even 50-minute chunks to allow yourself a substantial reset. Or consider scheduling a break proportionate with a meeting's duration so that you can have the necessary intermission and decompression before your next commitment.

Make meetings more impactful.

Often when we set meetings, we go into them with one set of objectives or ideas and another participant, understandably, comes in with their own. Expectations can be tricky because they're indicative of only one side of an equation. I've found that ensuring mutual agreements are in place with my counterparts prior to a meeting can help streamline communication and align goals for the meeting itself. While I believe in shortening meetings, I also believe in ensuring that the ones we do have function with the greatest efficacy possible. A quick e-mail exchange or pre-meeting with all parties around mutual agreements can make all the difference in the world, saving you time *and* energy.

> Do Less, Allow More

Have a balance between force and flow.

Every human being has masculine and feminine energy within them that is irrespective of gender. We associate masculine energy with functioning as the protector and the leader of the pack, while feminine energy is often tied to nurturing and creating life. Men have been associated with being less in touch with their feelings and therefore are typically attributed with rationality and logic as skill sets. Women have often been seen as more sensitive and open to exploring their feelings, but then they're unfairly labeled as irrational or emotional in both professional and personal settings. Consider this: If, symbolically, feminine energy is about nurturing and creation and masculine energy is associated with power and strength, perhaps our social conditioning has exploited this symbolism and played a large part in the imbalance we feel in this respect. Try taking stock of the ways in which you experience these different energies and notice how any imbalance can leave you with a persistent overcorrection in one direction or another.

Trust the universe.

Expect universal signs that confirm you are on your path. When I walked the Camino de Santiago, I saw markings that have guided millions of visitors who have sought "the Way" for centuries. And then there were the signs I could feel but not truly see in the physical sense of the word—the way the sun made me feel as it set on the horizon, the way I felt hugged by the limbs of a tree even when I wasn't touching them. Similarly, you will know the signs are off when you are met with resistance. This can be something seemingly insignificant, like when you keep hitting the Buy button but a website keeps crashing, or something more life-altering like losing your job or a partner leaving you. Look for signs affirming that you are aligned with your path and, just as importantly, the signs alerting you that you are off your path.

Become a channel for insights and guidance.

Open yourself up to the Universal Mind and all it has to offer. The energy you emit can either invite or discourage dialogue and support from others as well. One of the most rewarding parts of my coaching career is that the work with my clients becomes an exchange in vulnerability. We share in the collective wisdom of our wounds because we know that the process can be an inclusive, insightful endeavor that serves both the individual and the collective. Open your heart and mind to the ideas and experiences of the people around you. Be a safe place for others to express themselves and their ideas, and you will find that in return.

Tools

Energy Audit

One of the practical behaviors for the intention of leveraging energy over time is to take control of your own energy input and output. Becoming clear on what gives and takes from your energy is crucial for effective decision-making and maintaining healthy relationships.

Pick a week to perform an energy audit. Throughout this week, you'll track your daily activities and corresponding energy levels. Then you'll take stock of everything you've logged and evaluate what increases and decreases your energy.

Track everything that happens each day and color-code it according to the following priorities:

- LOVE (Self-Care, Partner, Family)
- GROW (Education, Reading, Developing Skills)
- SERVE (Volunteering, Impact, Mentoring)
- PLAY (Adventures, Hobbies, Social Activities)
- CREATE (Work, Creative Projects, Community)
- OTHER (Errands, Chores, Administrative Tasks)

1. Give each activity a rating of + or – based on your motivation, focus, and overall energy level during and after the activity. The plus indicates an overall positive experience, while the minus indicates an overall negative experience. Make a short note next to each activity identifying what factors contributed to your rating. Reflect on the day and make notes at the bottom of the sheet of things that may have impacted your overall energy. For example, being on technology first thing in the morning, drinking coffee late in the day, having an argument, restless sleep, etc.

2. Look for patterns where your energy is positive and where it is negative. Our energy field is penetrable, which means that we can control what we let in and out of it. What activities produce the most positivity? Which people are involved in those activities? Is there a pattern in the time of day when the more positive energies are flowing?

3. Identify when you're most energized, and optimize that time. You've likely discovered by now if you are a morning person or a night owl. Know your time of vitality and plan accordingly. For example, if you usually have a boost of energy midmorning, use that for creative work and your most important tasks.

4. Brainstorm how to mitigate your negatively rated activities. We may be programmed to believe we can do it all, but that programming is questionable at best. I believe we can have it all, but also that it comes with understanding the art of delegation and energy management. When possible, invest in someone to take things off your plate. Make that meeting shorter. Add more family time or increase the window you spend on wellness by waking up earlier.

5. After a week of tracking, optimize your calendar with color-coded categories. Use the suggested categories of *love, grow, serve, play, create,* and *other* to organize your commitments. Shorten or eliminate the activities you've given a negative rating. Add more of what you gave a positive rating. The simple, difficult truth is that if we don't control our calendar, someone else will. Take control of scheduling what matters to you—it will help you make decisions more efficiently and lead to attracting more positivity into your life.

Transition Process

With three simple steps, you can invite more Intentionality into your day anytime you are transitioning from one thing to another. This quick check-in will help you honor achievements, assess challenges, and mitigate risks throughout your day. It will give you insights into things you may be avoiding and also hold you accountable. Additionally, it will help you prioritize your task list.

1. Reflect on the role you've just been playing. Take a moment to reflect on what your previous role in the day has been and the environment you've been in. We rotate through many roles daily—parent, partner, friend, executive, mentor, volunteer, and so on, and we often bring the energy from a previous experience into the next. That's unfair to all involved. Take a moment to acknowledge your previous role. This is a great time to utilize the power of your breath.

2. Take note of the things you need to remember. Documenting outstanding thoughts or tasks enables you to free your mind from carrying these items into your next experience. Whether you use a digital app on your phone or computer, or jot things down the old-fashioned way, either will keep you focused and organized and prevent you from spending any unnecessary energy thinking that you might forget something.

3. Visualize the next role you will play. Visualize how you want to show up, and feel the emotions that would signify a fulfilling experience. See and feel yourself as a fully present being in the next environment. What would this entail? Perhaps it means you need to stop and pick up some groceries or flowers, or change your clothes to be more comfortable, or put your tech out of sight. For example, if you're coming from a fiery board meeting to your daughter's soccer game, you'll likely want to show up playful and supportive, not stressed and preoccupied. Recognize that your role and responsibilities will feel very different in each environment, and take ownership for being the person you aim to be.

Meeting Guide

One way to manage your energy effectively and set yourself up for successful interactions is to set agreements before every meeting. You can use this technique in the workplace and in your personal relationships. It will create an equilibrium of power by replacing expectations with agreements. Expectations are one-way and contribute to disillusionment, whereas agreements are mutually decided upon and create clarity for everyone involved.

Prior to any type of meeting, sit down with the other participant(s) and answer the following questions:

1. **What is the intention of this meeting?** Encourage the other person(s) to be very detailed in what they hope to get out of the meeting—and hold yourself to this same standard. I've found that this question has helped me garner a better understanding of our different perspectives and also to detect miscommunications earlier rather than later. Before moving on, get into agreement on the objectives for the meeting.

2. **What would success feel like at the end of this meeting?** This one is nuanced but very important. Typically, the question is worded, "What would success *look like* at the end of this meeting?" That's not what we're getting at here. Yes, I want you to identify the ideal outcome, but moreover, I want you to consider the outcome that would leave you and the other attendees feeling inspired, connected, and empowered. In my experience, getting this feedback for how everyone else hopes to experience the meeting has made me far more considerate, compassionate, and open-minded when coming to the table.

3. **What role do we each play in this meeting?** If you're a team leader, it's important to ask this question—not only of yourself, but particularly of the people you work with. You might envision yourself as the person leading the conversation, but it's very possible that another individual would like to have a greater voice or role in the decision-making process. This is true in relationships as well.

Oftentimes, we think our spouse wants us to offer solutions or fix the problem, but if we take a step back and ask them what role they need from us, we may find that it's less talking and more listening. An easy framework for addressing this question and not overcomplicating the response is to offer up these three options:

– **Listener/Sympathizer:** Your counterpart(s) just wants a friendly ear, someone they can vent to or brainstorm without repercussions or judgment. They want someone who can acknowledge and better understand their viewpoint.

– **Problem Solver/Coach:** Your counterpart(s) may want solutions. They may want you to ask more questions and help guide them to the heart of an issue. They may be looking for advice or ideas on how to bring resolution to the issue presented.

– **Creative Contributor:** Your counterpart(s) may want someone to lob ideas back and forth with. They may want a brainstorming session or collaborative effort to get their creative juices flowing.

4. **Do we have the right energy and environment to achieve this?** You know your mind and body better than anyone. Take a moment to consider how you entered the space. Are you carrying any unwanted energy from a prior circumstance? Are you feeling grounded and ready for a productive dialogue? And while you can never know fully what's transpiring within someone else, you can recognize an energy being emitted that may be less than optimal for an open conversation.

Also, assess your surroundings to determine whether the space feels conducive for the meeting. Remove as many distractors as possible, and don't underestimate the positive effect of aesthetics. Gaining a greater situational awareness of both your energy and your environment will enable you to ensure it's the right moment for this meeting. If it's not, reschedule and try again when all factors are better aligned.

If you take the time to sit down and address these four questions and find four mutual agreements, I promise you'll have a far more productive meeting. Even if the answers aren't what you expect, they help set the stage for better energetic alignment. In addition, I've found that everyone feels more seen and considered and less like an afterthought.

This meeting guide is something I even refer to in the back of my mind in impromptu discussions. That's because these four simple questions can help reset the energy in any given situation. Without fail, if you do the same, you'll eventually establish a more consistent way to manage your energy in all of your relationships.

KEY TAKEAWAYS

Behaviors for Leveraging Energy

- Evaluate what increases and decreases your energy.
- Learn to regulate your own energy.
- Learn to protect your energy.
- Take charge of your day.
- Do less, allow more.

Tools for Leveraging Energy

- Energy Audit
- Transition Process
- Meeting Guide

CHAPTER 9

EMBRACING DISCIPLINE

Discipline gets a bad rap. And that's because, as I've noted, the most popular understanding and widely used meaning of the word is "punishment as a form of teaching." After growing up in a house where physical force was touted as an acceptable form of discipline, and after my career in the Australian military, I began to challenge the conventional wisdom around this idea.

Was it possible that because we've lived and worked in cultures that have rooted themselves in fear for centuries, discipline became bastardized in its intent? How and why had it become the most favorable deterrent for behavior that our systems deemed problematic or threatening?

For as far back as I can remember, I had confused discipline with rigidity—with staying in line so I didn't get beaten, reprimanded, or put in detention. In many respects, as a young man, my actions were based far more on fear of what would happen to me or were acts of rebellion against the rigid systems that never seemed to give me the benefit of the doubt.

I wish someone had told me what I'm about to tell you—discipline is not about consequences. It's about consistency. Discipline is focusing on your intentions, not your failures. This chapter highlights the behaviors and tools that will empower you to identify how you want to feel and to maintain a lifestyle that consistently supports that.

Behaviors

Practice Daily Routines

Adopt a morning routine.

When you wake up in the morning, you naturally move from a delta to a beta brain wave state. But the trajectory here can often be misleading. The problem for most people is that they skip the interim states and jump to beta straight away—which is not what you want to do. When you first wake up, you automatically move from delta into theta. You then want to optimize the next period from theta to alpha, and then ideally stay in your alpha state during your morning routine. Think of this as the first chance in your day to be still, establish inner peace, and generate both an equilibrium and a manageable pace with which to move throughout your day.

Your first step as you awaken is to leverage the theta state and impress onto the subconscious what you want to bring into your life. This is as simple as setting an intention to feel a particular way and then envisioning yourself moving through the day in ways that lead to that feeling. (This is also an ideal place from which to practice the scientific manifestation process, which you'll learn about in Part V). Then as you transition into the alpha state, you can embark on your morning routine while remaining calm. This empowers you to claim the day, set the tone on your terms, and ensure that you remain intentional with the energy you're putting in motion.

Do something rather than nothing.

One idea I believe serves everyone is Voltaire's aphorism that "perfect is the enemy of good." I love using this as a mantra because it gets at the heart of so many well-intentioned missteps I've both experienced myself and witnessed in my clients. At home, I have a lengthy and robust morning routine, but sometimes when I'm traveling, I work late nights and start early the next day—which limits the capacity I may have for my routine. I generally choose to prioritize sleep, which may leave me with a shorter window for a morning routine, but ultimately it is better for my overall state. Don't lose sight of the feeling you get with small, incremental changes that can lead to lasting transformation. To achieve your desired feelings, remember that you don't need perfection—you only need progress.

Adopt an evening routine.

Much like your first moments of the day, the period just before falling asleep is when the subconscious is most impressionable. This moment also corresponds with the greatest opportunity to create. This means you need to be very intentional about how you prepare yourself for experiencing it optimally. You need to intentionally let go of the day and of anything that didn't go the way you would have liked.

Start to wind down at least an hour before you plan to crawl into bed, and allow for the same transition period as the morning brain wave state but in the opposite order. Drop out of the high-paced beta state and into the alpha state, where you can relax with a cup of tea, meditation, or nighttime stroll. Then get into bed and allow yourself to get drowsy as you drop into theta state and toward dreamland, where the subconscious creates.

Plan, but Be Willing to Pivot

Be gentle with yourself.

Life is going to throw you curveballs. Every path has a challenging period of time where you will reckon with the reality that our own best-laid plans are not always what's best for us in the end. The inertia you may feel during a pivot is natural—because your new direction is ripe for comparison to the illusions that likely have been in your system for quite some time. Give yourself some space and grace to recode. Because when you leave behind the image of what your life was supposed to look like, you allow for the unlimited possibilities of what it can become.

Focus on agreements, not expectations.

Expectations are a messy thing. I had a friend once say that they're "predetermined disappointments." I've heard of them referred to as "premeditated resentments." I don't disagree with either, but my biggest issue with expectations is that they've never once served me or anyone I love. And I've come to the conclusion that the reason these conversations don't serve any of us is because they are one-way. They are illusions. Agreements require mutual participation and can always be adapted.

Avoid making assumptions.

Assumptions are a very self-centered approach and are based on what we believe to be true—which, as you've learned from all of this talk about negative belief loops, can often be misguided. Ask, don't assume. When possible, give the benefit of the doubt. By avoiding assumptions, you can eliminate unnecessary stress and anxiety—in both the short and long term. This simple act could save you a lot of frustration and energy.

Build and Keep the Momentum

Beware of too much focus on the "big picture."

Sometimes when we let our mind run the full spectrum of the task at hand, we can get easily overwhelmed. Of course, there's nothing wrong with having a 30,000-foot view of what you're hoping to do, but the best odds of making that dream a reality are in the thousands of baby steps you take along the way. After my divorce, there were days when I could not find the strength to get out of bed. Not only was it difficult for me to envision my life six months down the line, it was difficult for me to envision how I was going to make it through the next six hours. The small steps I took for myself that helped me find fleeting feelings of peace, love, and joy made all the difference. I focused on eating well, sleeping, walking, journaling, doing acts of kindness, meditation, and more. Find the little things that create a positive trajectory in your day and do them incrementally.

Take comfort in knowing there are many paths to the same destination.

When I met my former wife, I envisioned our lives together, forever. I pictured the business we would build, the adventures we would take, and the home we would make our own. That didn't pan out. But the path I did take through feeling heartbreak and grief and loss has brought me out on the other side—and to a beautiful partner with whom I've built another life, business, and home: a reality that is more fulfilling and nourishing than I could have ever dreamed of. Remember that there is no one path. If you remember that life is circular and that progress rarely moves in a straight line, you'll know that you're capable of connecting dots from anywhere you may find yourself and carving a path of your own.

Ask yourself, *Is this increasing or decreasing my momentum?*

Ask this question, and ask it often. This is how you can distinguish between being rigid and being disciplined, and will help you make more efficient decisions. Momentum, even in the smallest forms, means progress. Maybe what you're doing isn't how you thought you'd be spending your day, but it is playing a helpful role in how you want to feel. Maybe it's still moving the needle, just not at the pace that you envisioned. As long as it's serving you—to any degree—that's momentum. That's still discipline. And that's more than enough.

Leverage Systems and Technology

Make your own accountability infrastructure.

Create colors or labels associated with the different types of commitments on your personal calendar. As discussed, I recommend doing this in line with the five priorities: *love, grow, serve, play,* and *create.* That way you can streamline the scheduling process and align it with your priorities, including those on a family or shared workplace calendar. This is not unlike what you do in an energy audit, but you're applying it across the board in perpetuity. This process will enable you to visually see how balanced—or unbalanced—your calendar is. It will also embolden you to make space for vacations, self-care, and free time—the things that often get cut. If something is in your calendar, honor that you've committed to the event, but if other things come up (as they often do), allow for it to move to another date or time.

"Do not disturb."

As much as I might want to slow things down, society and technology will always continue to evolve, and as such, they aim to make things more efficient (translation: faster). I can't change the pace of technology—but I can change myself. And so can you. And that starts with the story you're telling yourself about hyperconnectivity.

We all have smartphones and constant 24/7 access to information. But our bodies are not designed to interface with them at all moments of the day. In other words, our bodies are not meant to be connected at all times. We often believe that if our phone is off, we'll miss something important, and that if we missed something important, it was avoidable and a consequence of being disconnected. But disconnection can be the beginning of a new story of self-discipline, presence, and satisfaction. Use your do-not-disturb features. Put your phone on airplane mode. Draw technological boundaries and choose digital hygiene that supports how you want to feel.

Make technology your friend, not your foe.

I can't tell you the number of times I've heard a friend say, "I lost my phone and it's just been awful," only to hear another friend chime in and say, "I wish that happened to me." I've been in both positions. I was also on an airplane recently where the Wi-Fi wasn't working. And you know what my thought was? *What a relief! I can have some time to myself.*

Anxiety accompanies our devices. Having the connection is both a gift and a curse. Looking at stories and reels on Instagram, scrolling on X (formerly Twitter) or TikTok, and refreshing our inboxes, an hour can go by without us realizing it. But how do you feel when you find yourself doing these things? For me, I feel an emptiness when there's no intention behind how I'm using an app or a piece of technology. I start feeling like I only engaged with it out of habit or codependency—and I feel like I've lost my agency over the device and my relationship with it.

But we can course correct. We're able to take ownership of how we want to feel about the devices we use and establish boundaries for intentionally engaging with technology. Whether it's connecting with friends, finding new ways to share your expertise with the world, or learning a new skill, prioritize using tech for only things that will bring you more peace, love, and joy.

Keep Your Critic in Check

Avoid shame motivation.

Striving for perfection instead of progress can trigger feelings of shame. Oftentimes, we use shame to drive us toward our goal because we believe that when we reach it, we can eradicate a negative feeling from our body. That's just not true. Once we bring shame spirals into our belief loops, we are operating from a fear state. In the past, I shamed myself when earlier businesses of mine did not go the way I wanted them to. I connected the loss of money with a loss of capability and spent a long time shaming myself for the decisions that had led to temporary financial stress. Shame didn't help me make that money back. It just triggered me to stay further mired in the mess. What helped me recover both the money and my sense of self-worth were positive incentives—identifying how I wanted to feel and taking incremental steps toward making that a reality. You can avoid shame motivation by focusing on gradual benchmarks and feelings of pride.

Acknowledge your achievements.

Is it nice to be honored or recognized by our peers or loved ones? Of course. But dignity can be a beautiful, solo act that's even more powerful when derived from within. When you stop to recognize what you've accomplished, you not only show yourself love and respect, but you also attract more opportunities.

One tendency that we have as humans is constantly looking for what's better. This can help us to keep things from becoming stagnant or mediocre. But the downside of this need for progress is often feeling like we're not doing well enough or that we're not good enough. When we are constantly seeking, we're keeping ourselves in a low-vibrational state. A practice that you can do to combat this is to habitually write down what you're doing and the progress you've made. Ask yourself, *What are the things that are going well in my life, and how are they making me feel?*

You will then have a running document of all the wonderful things you have in your life and all the achievements you're proud of. Whenever you're feeling a little bit low, go back to this list and remind yourself, *Yes, I might be having a bad day. But look at what incredible progress I've made and what achievements I've had.* Just that simple act will help you stop the negative spiral and remind you that you're exactly where you need to be.

Build defenses.

Inner critics are always lingering in our internal world. And the ego is always on hyperdrive in our external world trying to protect us—it's constantly looking for ways to justify its existence and will bring you down when you're most vulnerable.

This means that we must be prepared to overpower these tricky menaces when they arise. I know that when I travel, I sometimes worry that I'll be out of shape by the time I get home or that I'll have gained a few pounds. By the end of the trip, I've built up so much self-judgment that it eclipses the joy and the memories I just created. Knowing I can fall prey to this, I remind myself that my long-term progress is on track, that I'm healthy and fit, and that I'll reset and take greater care of myself when I get home. I know that I can rely on the evidence of my own actions to override the inner critic and the ego, who always seem to have an opinion. Don't feel the need to justify relaxation or indulgences. Experiences don't always need to be rationalized or explained. Avoid the inclination to shame yourself for any steps off your path and instead have faith that you'll eventually get back in the rhythm of a routine that inspires and serves you.

Tools

Morning Routine

The morning sets the tone for your entire day. When you make the switch from sleeping to waking, you have the opportunity to choose to be the master of your mind.

Creating a morning routine that is customized to you is important, because it means you'll adhere to it. Here are some recommended ways to start your day with Intentionality, but of course, get creative and do what best works for you:

- **Set your intention for the day.** Do this while you're still in bed, as soon as you start to become consciously aware. Place a smile on your face for 17 seconds and set an intention for the day. The physical act of smiling will code your mind to believe you're happy from the second you wake up. Then, identify your desired feelings for the day. Pick three positive feelings and visualize your day playing out in the best way possible. Finally, identify what specific behaviors will help you achieve these feelings and commit to doing these with intention.

- **Drink eight ounces of hot water with fresh-squeezed lemon and a quarter teaspoon of Himalayan sea salt.** This is good for activating your system without having the rise and crash that caffeine causes. It also has an alkaline effect, bringing the body back to neutrality by reducing its acidity.

- **Go outside and get sunlight into your eyes for 10 to 30 minutes after waking up.** This is a way to synchronize your body's rhythm to that of Mother Nature. It's best to do this when the sun is rising, but not imperative. Take time to engage with the natural light, going for a morning stroll or enjoying a hot drink outdoors. Try to refrain from checking technology in this time.

- **Do some breathwork.** Taking some conscious breaths will have tremendous benefits regardless of how long or short your session is. You can find many guided sessions on the Intentionality app, available in both the Google Play and Apple stores.

- **Meditate in a style that works for you.** Meditation can take on many forms: silent, chanting, walking, or a guided session. The important thing about meditation is not how you do it, just that you keep coming back to the present moment.

- **Do some movement.** Qigong, yoga, or kundalini are great for awakening and stretching the body, but any form of movement will get your energy moving and kick-start your feel-good hormones.

- **Journal.** Any form of reflection is beneficial. A simple formula is to note your intention for the day, create a positive belief loop that will support that intention, and jot down three expressions of gratitude.

- **Read something positive.** While I read a large variety of material, here are my top five books that I have on continuous rotation:

  Tao Te Ching by Lao-tzu
  A New Earth by Eckhart Tolle
  The Four Agreements by Don Miguel Ruiz
  Meditations by Marcus Aurelius
  A Course in Miracles by Helen Schucman

- **Make a nourishing breakfast and eat it while journaling, reading, spending quality time with family and/or friends, or enjoying some alone time.** Providing yourself nourishment can be a very soothing and self-loving act. By carving out the space for this and delineating it from the rigorous pace of the day ahead, you can enjoy this sacred time and demonstrate how to care for yourself before giving your energy to others.

Evening Routine

Don't sleep on it—pun intended—discover an evening routine that works for you! Intentionally shutting yourself down is, quite literally, an essential part of building yourself up. The list of actions that follows is what I use for my daily evening routine. See what appeals to you, and make adjustments to accommodate your needs and schedule so that is it more likely you will adhere to it.

- **Complete the Intentionality Transition Process (found on pages 167–168).** This tool will help you assess your achievements and challenges and help you prepare for the tasks you want to prioritize tomorrow. Following the steps will also give you insights into the issues you may be avoiding and hold you accountable to showing up as the best version of yourself.

- **Close down all work-related browsers on your computer and either turn it off or put it in sleep mode at the end of your workday.** When possible, make an intentional cut-off time for your workday and hold yourself accountable to it. This way, if you decide to use your computer for something else the rest of the day, you avoid the temptation of slipping back into work mode.

- **Go outside and get sunlight into your eyes for 10 to 30 minutes before sunset.** Just like in your morning routine, this is not a call to action for you to look directly into the sun. It's simply getting you outside into the healing powers of nature and engaging with natural light. The setting of the sun will clue your body in to its natural circadian rhythm.

- **Dim the lights in your home after sunset.** Think of this the way you have the screen dimmer on your phone. Dim the lights as the evening progresses and if you're really committed, use only candlelight for the final hour before bed. The idea is to taper off your light intake and promote relaxation.

- **When possible, eat dinner around 6 P.M. and limit your intake of liquids thereafter.** Timing may not always be exact, but the intent here is to start preparing your body for sleep mode. Limiting your intake of liquids as the night goes on prevents you from having to use the bathroom after lying down for sleep.

- **Wind down from technology a minimum of one hour before you go to sleep.** When possible, put your phone on airplane mode from 9 P.M. to 9 A.M. to avoid the temptation of habitual use. This will also help you start dropping into the slower brain wave states of alpha and theta.

- **Go to sleep when you first start feeling sleepy.** Do not push through the sleepy state. If you do, your body instinctively activates the next circadian rhythm—which means that you're missing the window of falling asleep with ease.

Conscious Tech Use

Do you become anxious anytime your phone is not on you? Do you find yourself endlessly refreshing your inbox? Are you forever "just glancing" at social media? It's tempting to blame the tech revolution for the far-reaching ways our lives have changed in the past two decades. We're more connected than ever, but we're lonelier too. Our attention spans are now officially less than a goldfish's because it's the only way we can cope with the constant onslaught of information. But technology is not the problem—the problem is that we've allowed it to control our lives.

Here are some ways to create a conscious and intentional relationship with technology:

- **Do not go online first thing in the morning—and definitely not while in bed.** You create new neurons every night, and they need a positive feeding ground. As soon as you expose yourself to the digital world, you're exposing your energy field to others' opinions, priorities, and mindsets—which is to say, you're starting your day by diverting your energy to reactionary measures instead of reclaiming it for your own benefit. Be diligent about setting aside some time to wake up before diving into the digital world.

- **Set virtual boundaries.** Start making it a routine to check e-mail on your terms. One way to reduce your inbox time is to do only midmorning and midafternoon check-ins. This forces you to prioritize your task list and reduces the risk of unpredictable things hijacking your energy. You can also manage expectations of your response time by putting on an away message letting people know your "online" hours.

- **Integrate Intentionality practices into your day.** Many of us have switched to technology for things like journaling and reading. Although many of these systems are extremely innovative, I encourage you to rethink where you may be potentially sacrificing benefits for convenience. Make sure you also schedule regular breaks throughout your day to rest your eyes, engage in some movement, and get some fresh air. Scheduling them into your calendar will make it more likely that they happen—and challenge yourself to leave your phone behind.

- **Filter your consumption.** Your belief loops are heavily influenced by social media and the digital world. The people who created these systems have implemented algorithms that create addictions to your feeds. To take back control, you must be intentional about what you allow into your energy field. Much like when we limit media intake for children, you must consider what creates negative feelings and be aware of what you're exposing yourself to. Do a social media cleanse and follow only influencers and accounts that encourage positive thoughts and behaviors.

- **Say no to tech at the table.** Make it a practice to have *no* phones at the table. Even when a phone is face down, the temptation is too strong. Out of sight is out of mind. Additionally, encourage your family and friends to put phones away as soon as you sit down for a meal, tea or coffee date, or any social gathering. You'll face resistance, but the benefits of pure presence will be worth it.

- **Have an intentional evening routine.** One of the best ways to sabotage your sleep is to watch TV, play video games, or engage in stressful work near bedtime—they will all influence your dreaming state. Ideally, switch off all screens two hours before bed, or one hour at the very least. Blue-blocking glasses may help minimize the effect of screens, but an even better solution is to eliminate screen time at night, set your devices to night mode, and turn off all push notifications.

- **Commit to a weekly cyber sabbath.** This means no computer, no iPads, no phones, and so on for 24 hours straight. Give your friends and family a heads-up about your offline time so they don't worry—it might just inspire them to adopt the practice too.

  It's equally important to prepare for your return to the digital world before logging back on. Choose the time when you'll turn your phone/computer/WiFi back on, and make sure you're in a calm state when that time comes.

KEY TAKEAWAYS

Behaviors for Embracing Discipline

- Practice daily routines.
- Plan, but be willing to pivot.
- Build and keep the momentum.
- Leverage systems and technology.
- Keep your inner critic in check.

Tools for Embracing Discipline

- Morning Routine
- Evening Routine
- Conscious Tech Use

CHAPTER 10

CHOOSING LOVE

Here's the bottom line. We've been conditioned to feel fear much more than to feel love. As I've shown throughout this book, fear is a deeply embedded emotion that is a cultural construct, a lucrative business, and a critical component of our subconscious coding. But guess what? It's also not a foregone conclusion.

With a renewed focus on behaviors and tools that equip you for a manual override, it is not only possible to conquer your fears, it is possible to choose love as a permanent intention at the heart—quite literally—of a better quality of life.

This chapter provides you with the resources to forgo fear in favor of love. The behaviors and tools that follow reinforce the notion that choosing love is one of the most effective ways to find and sustain your inner peace.

Behaviors

Make heart coherence a priority.

The heart is the source of wisdom, insight, and intuition. Think of it as the mecca of inner peace. Tapping into this part of your body and its rhythmic relationship with your breath can put you on the path to acceptance and to having greater compassion for yourself and others. I like to think of the heart as fear's kryptonite. Fear is a negative force that can paralyze us into inaction and then propel us into downward spirals and further negative belief loops. But in the presence of true heart coherence, as you might recall from Chapter 1, it becomes weakened and eventually irrelevant in our system.

Take advantage of your superpower.

Speaking of the power of heart coherence, even just your breath—you typically take more than 20,000 breaths in a day—is its own superpower. Our breath gives us the chance to observe our beliefs, behaviors, and feelings, which means we have more than 20,000 chances a day to decide if we want to continue with or change the state we are in. Reclaiming our relationship with our breath is how we reclaim our relationship with ourselves.

There's a reason I've referred to breath exercises as "circuit breakers." You're the only one who can prevent yourself from short-circuiting, and you're the only one who can reset the way forward. Have you ever stopped and considered why someone facing an uphill, often frightening task ahead, is told, "Just breathe," or "Take a breath, you've got this"? This is a reminder that in critical moments, breath is where you can take back agency over your body and your behaviors. If fear is getting the best of you, and you feel yourself spinning or spiraling into your negative belief loops, you don't have to know the whole road map for escaping the cycle.

You just have to focus on the heart-centered act of activating your superpower and taking the first breath forward.

Ask your heart rather than your head.

According to the National Institutes of Health (NIH) and the HeartMath Institute,[1] the heart sends more information to the brain than the other way around. An NIH study to explore whether pain resides in a person's brain or in their heart mentions that "the heart has its 'little brain' or 'intrinsic cardiac nervous system.' This 'heart brain' is composed of approximately 40,000 neurons that are like neurons in the brain, meaning that the heart has its own nervous system."[2] The study also states, "Research has demonstrated that pain perception is modulated by neural pathways and methods targeting the heart such as vagus nerve stimulation and heart-rhythm coherence feedback techniques." The study ultimately concluded that "the heart is probably a key moderator of pain."[3]

When I first read this, I felt validated. I've struggled with chronic injuries and pain in my neck, back, and shoulders for many years. A nonnegotiable part of my preventive and corrective self-care is focused on navigating pain by beginning with what I'm feeling in my heart. I meditate. I do breathing exercises. I focus on what I'm feeling "in here" rather than "out there" first. And I don't think it's a coincidence that when I learned to feel my way through the pain rather than adopting a "mind over matter" mentality of persevering, I was able to heal myself more effectively.

> Reaffirm the Belief that Life Is Happening for You, Not to You

Create your own prayer.

Let me clarify that religion is not a prerequisite here; I use the word *prayer* to describe a statement or declaration from my higher self. Find or create a divine prayer that inspires you and connects you to the Universal Mind, and then read it each morning and evening. The Universal Mind, as we've discovered, is the highest form of energy, and it's something omnipresent that we are all connected to. Since prayer can mean different things to different people, find an expression that tethers you to this infinite energy field and explore the language that resonates for you. I've found that a collection of "I am" statements can be very powerful for reminding a person of their infinite power on both a conscious and subconscious level.

Remember the law of polarity.

Positivity does not exist without negativity. Negativity is real, but there are ways to navigate it with an optimistic or abundant mindset. Consider what the negative situation is teaching you.

For example, when I'm focusing on changing my diet, particularly after a trip of indulging in heavier entrees or lots of unconscious snacking, it's easy for me to feel that I'm about to enter into a journey full of restrictions. My thoughts go to *I now can't have that for dinner*, or *I shouldn't have any dessert*. But I've found that countering that negativity by focusing on what I can *add* to my routine instead of on what's being taken away changes my whole mindset. When I explore a new recipe or cook in a different style than usual, I begin feeling less constrained and find myself looking forward to the fact that I'm cooking something healthy that I've never tried before.

Another way to apply the law of polarity is to look back at your greatest difficulties and see how they were always the parts of your life where you grew the most. Moments of struggle are often when new opportunities come into your life or when you learn a new skill. When you find yourself in a challenging experience, see if you can perceive how the negative aspect is part of a larger, dualistic whole. When you connect to the law of polarity, you realize the necessary dualities that are being presented to you and remember that you're capable of transcending this moment. In doing so, you'll be able to embrace the current situation, change your energetic state, and move into action.

Reflect on the challenges.

Often when we're struggling through a crisis, trauma, or simply a frustrating problem, we're unable to see through the weeds and are only capable of feeling or identifying the negatives. I've always said that there's a big difference between living in the past and learning from it. That's because I firmly believe you can revisit a situation and rewrite the story you're telling yourself by reflecting and writing down what you've learned. Ask yourself how the experience has shaped you in positive ways and how it proved to be a valuable cautionary tale that has led to better personal decision-making in your present.

Forgive Yourself and Others

Make a list of everyone you need to forgive.

Forgiveness is an important part of feeling free and functioning in an optimal state. After being estranged from my father for 18 years, I spent some time clarifying what I needed—both from him and from myself—to move forward in our relationship. I needed to be able to forgive myself for all the years I'd allowed the pain of our relationship to overshadow how I lived. I needed to forgive him for the abuse in my childhood. It was less about hearing specific admissions or vocal examples of accountability from him and more about forging the conversation itself.

You will know you need to forgive someone if you feel any feelings of resentment or ill-will toward them and when you are unable to think of the person without thinking of the hurt they've caused you. Identify what you need to forgive yourself and others for and write it down, detailing the negative feelings you've been holding on to. And remember that while mutual understanding in the matter is not guaranteed, it's also not necessary. That's because forgiveness can be a one-way avenue—one designed to reinstate *your* inner peace, not necessarily the inner peace of the person or group of people you're forgiving.

Decide what kind of forgiveness is needed.

Often you may find that you don't need to engage with anyone else to go through the acts of forgiveness. You can decide whether you need to address the other person or group of people, or if you would prefer to resolve the issue with a letting-go ceremony on your own. Either way is powerful, but if you decide to do it solo, you could try honoring the process with one of these practices:

- **Write a letter and then burn it.** This ceremony allows me to express every unfiltered emotion coursing through my body, regardless of how dark or painful, and it empowers me to release them into the ether. Take the time to feel the words and emotions you put on that page, and let them go back into the earth, trusting they will be neutralized and dissolved. You'll be able to leave any fears about confrontation behind and move forward buoyed with love.

- **Do a cord-cutting meditation.** Rest flat on the ground, preferably directly on the earth, and imagine the ties that connect you to the person you want to forgive. Imagine yourself using a giant pair of scissors to cut the ties while embracing bright, healing light from above. Feel yourself untether from any lingering negativity. Let the light shine into any dark or empty place inside and surrender to the healing energies, releasing yourself fully into this act of forgiveness.

- **Hold a cacao ceremony.** Cacao ceremonies are an ancient ritual from the Olmec civilization and are used for opening your heart and tuning in to creative guidance. I do cacao ceremonies regularly as a way to connect with myself and use the spirit of cacao to help me overcome any form of resistance I may be experiencing. This is my regular reminder that there is always more to feel, and that with every fear I release and with every forgiveness I can offer, there is more love I can give to myself and others.

To do a ceremony, make sure you source organically grown and ethically produced cacao. (Note: this isn't typically found in supermarkets, even the natural ones.) Prepare the cacao while being fully present and connect to an area in your life where you would like to give or receive more love. You can enjoy cacao alone or share with others. It will enhance whatever you're doing and bring you into greater connectivity to the Universal Mind. This sacred practice will help you transcend limiting beliefs, experience your feelings, and reignite your inner spark.

Free yourself by releasing low-vibrational energies.

Resentment, blame, and victimhood are synonymous with low-vibrational forces and finite energy sources. When you don't forgive, you allow fear to sabotage your relationships and take up space within your body and your consciousness. But when you release these energies, you can reclaim your power, lend compassion to yourself and others, and remind yourself that we are always works in progress. You can use palo santo or sage for this energetic release. Allow the smoke to flow over you to cleanse and burn away any negative energy.

Another way to release negative energies is to do a saltwater bath with some apple cider vinegar. Light a candle or some incense and close your eyes as you imagine cleansing yourself of all negative energy. This process can also be as simple as taking a shower and imagining washing away the impurities and toxins you've encountered. Nighttime showers are particularly helpful in this regard—in many cultures around the world, night bathing has been historically more prominent as a way to cleanse any negative energy from the day.

Know Where You Stand

Identify the impacts of others' behaviors.

Take stock of your relationships. Just as you've learned in the Energy Audit, it's worth looking at who makes you feel seen, understood, and loved—and just as importantly, who instigates feelings of fear, contempt, or shame. This will give you the opportunity to draw boundaries on how much energy you spend with those individuals. When you spend energy on fear-based relationships, you engender fear-based results. When you give of yourself to people who are effusive with their love, you are mutually contributing to a higher vibration.

A key component here is to be compassionate with yourself when assessing the impacts of others on your energetic field. Once you identify that someone is a consistent energy deterrent, it can be very confronting—and it also doesn't mean you necessarily *need* to confront them. My advice is not to slink away or ignore the person. Show up with love, and you'll know whether sharing your observations with the person is worth it or whether it's best kept as an internal lesson you can carry with you. Ask yourself what you hope to achieve by telling them what you've observed and identified about how their behavior affects you. And then ask yourself if the conversation is coming from a place of ego and needing to be right, or one that's an invitation to a more loving and honest relationship. In many cases, especially where there's an existing rift or growing distance, resolving your pain independently is sometimes more than enough and better supports your personal capacity.

Give people the opportunity to understand you.

Intellect isn't going to translate to intimacy. The best way to give someone the opportunity to understand you is to share from your heart. The greatest connections happen when you share your feelings vulnerably and regularly. Try putting yourself out there by telling a story you haven't traditionally shared. This will serve as an invitation to others and show that you're willing and capable of navigating their pain or their triumph with as much delicacy as you do your own.

Ask others for insights.

It's important to ask other people how you can show up for them. Take a moment to consider what questions might make the other person feel included and how asking them for their insights might serve as a powerful gateway for better understanding how they've personally experienced your behaviors. An open dialogue designed to gather insights into others' perspectives will remind them that you value honesty and that you can hold a safe space for vulnerability or difficult conversations.

Use Acknowledgment as a Gift

Make a list of acknowledgments.

Acknowledgment is the ultimate gift of recognition. It fosters deep levels of connection because people feel loved when they feel seen. What have you needed to hear from someone else? What has someone else, perhaps, been longing to hear from you? Offering acknowledgments to yourself is an act of self-love. Offering acknowledgments to others shows that you're willing to leave your ego, judgments, and limiting beliefs behind. We all deserve to be recognized in the light of love.

Reflect on your relationships.

We all have relationships where, at one point or another, we've felt a disconnect or a lack of intimacy. This is an opportunity for you to identify how your behaviors may have contributed to the other person's perception or experience of the situation. Write them an acknowledgment letter and send it—or don't send it and simply use it to explore in greater detail the roles each of us play in creating distance.

I've personally found that when I've written a letter like this, taking ownership has been both effective and empowering. For example, I once wrote a letter to a friend intending to initiate an honest conversation about the reasons why so much time had passed since last we'd spoken. The more time that passed, the harder it felt to write the letter. However, once I did, I made an intentional, deliberate effort to take ownership by saying, "I feel . . ." instead of, "You made me feel . . ." and "There is a distance between us, and I want to apologize for my part in how long this has continued," instead of, "You don't seem to care that this much time has passed."

When you put yourself in the other person's shoes and show awareness of how your words or actions may have hurt them, you demonstrate personal ownership and sincere consideration for the other person. You're also more likely to bridge the gap or, at the very least, find peace in knowing your efforts were rooted in compassion and a willingness to rekindle the love in your life.

Initiate conscious conversations.

Conflict is part of our earthly existence. You are human, and your beliefs, thoughts, and behaviors do not always align with others' mindsets and choices. But accepting that conflict is a part of life is not the same thing as allowing it to be a permanent emotional energy field between two parties. Conflicts will persist when you're more invested in what you fear about the other person or entity rather than what you can do to transform the relationship. Reflect on how you could give the other party the benefit of the doubt or what could have been the more loving perspective. Ask yourself what you need and then relay this in a calm, clear way—never presuming that the need will be met. Realize that sometimes, you'll need to let things go without the resolution you think you need.

Tools

Forgiveness and Acknowledgment

Forgiveness is a powerful way to reinstate your inner peace. It's less about the person or people you're forgiving, and mutual understanding in the matter is not guaranteed or necessary. Forgiveness offers the gift of freedom—whether it's forgiving another person or forgiving yourself, you are liberating yourself from energies that no longer serve you and are likely holding you back.

Acknowledgment is a gift and fosters deeper levels of connection. People feel loved when they feel seen—and that can include seeing and honoring yourself. When you do this for others, it should be an altruistic act without an expectation of receiving anything in return. Acknowledgment offers the gift of recognition and is a gesture of unconditional love.

Don't underrate the power and relevance of this act, even if it's been years since you've last been in touch with someone. This intentional outreach can create a snowball effect and change your relationships in ways beyond what you can imagine.

1. Make a list of everything you need to forgive yourself for and everything you need to forgive others for.

2. Write a forgiveness letter detailing the lessons you learned from an event and how they've shaped you in positive ways. Rather than remaining the victim of the situation, describe how you want to feel moving forward and how you will release the negative feelings you have been holding on to. It is not necessary to send the letter, check in with your heart to see what the best course of action is for you.

3. Make a list of everything you'd like acknowledgment for and everyone you can give acknowledgment to.

4. Reach out to the people on your acknowledgment list and share what you've written. It can be a note of appreciation or acknowledgment for something you would have liked to do differently if you'd had the chance.

Communication Method

This is a method you can use in any type of conflict that may arise. Once you start to notice tension building, it's best to take a few minutes to process your role in the conflict and any reactions you may be having.

Although they may seem minute, little bits of resentment can build over time and eventually turn into huge disruptors. Any time something gives you an emotional charge, no matter how small, it's your responsibility to either clear it or communicate to the other person so they're aware of how it's affecting you.

When you feel regulated and that you can reengage with the other person in a positive way, use the following five steps to help move through difficult emotions with ownership rather than projection—and ultimately ask for what you need.

1. **Introduction.** Introduce the situation with only the facts. The point here is to make sure you're both recalling the same situation. Remember, our egos are likely highly activated at this point, and our opinions can sneak in. Do your best to describe the triggering moment without using biased language.

2. **Feelings.** Describe how the situation made you feel. This is the time to focus on "I" rather than "you" statements. Feelings should be described in one word—like sad, rejected, disappointed, etc.

3. **Story.** Share the story you're telling yourself about the situation. For example, "The story I'm telling myself is that my ideas don't matter and aren't received as valuable input." Our stories sabotage our experiences.

This is the chance to be honest and vulnerable about how you may be your own unreliable narrator. Take ownership and try to avoid accusing the other person of making you feel a certain way.

4. **Needs.** Identify your needs, and be as specific as possible. An example of this is, "I need confirmation that you've received my e-mail and that you'll take time to review my proposal by the end of today." If you're unsure of your needs, consider what you were hoping to get from the other person before the conflict ensued. What will leave you feeling seen, accepted and valued?

5. **Invitation.** Ask the other person, without expectation, if they would be willing to do what you've requested. It always helps to use an affectionate nickname or some humor to bring lightheartedness to what may be an otherwise emotionally charged situation. The other party's cooperation is not guaranteed, but it's highly likely they'll want to meet your needs if they're presented in a calm and intentional manner.

Here's an example of how I used this method in my relationship with my partner:

Introduction: *Remember the other day when I left early for skiing with Mike and you commented, "Have fun without me . . ."*
Feelings: *I felt guilty, sad, and unappreciated.*
Story: *The story I'm telling myself is that you want me to dampen my excitement and enjoyment when you're not involved in my adventures.*
Needs: *What I need is for you to recognize the times I do ski with you and be happy for me when I have the opportunity to go on my own adventures—and please forego the passive-aggressive comments.*
Invitation: *Would you be willing to do that for me, honey bunches of oats?*

Conflict Playbook

Being conflict averse or non-confrontational can often lead to un-resolved feelings, destructive patterns, and a cycle of divisiveness. I created the Conflict Playbook to provide a simple formula to use when I'm triggered and likely in a reactive mode. Following this process allows you the opportunity to have a pattern-interrupt when emotions are running high and to reground yourself physically and emotionally to a state of love when an inevitable conflict ensues. Make sure to do the following six steps in order to ensure that you are operating from a place of Intentionality:

1. **Identify that you're actively in a conflict.**
    Identifying a conflict is not as simple as it sounds. To identify where friction lies between two or more people or groups of people is hard to do through the lens of objectivity. Almost always, even the description of the problem at hand is colored by one of the parties involved in perpetuating it, so do your best to stay neutral about why or how the conflict has arisen and simply call out that you are all in a heightened state.

2. **Remind yourself that shutting down is not an option.** You owe your complete presence to yourself and the others involved in the conflict. Don't run away or use the avoidant phrase "It's fine." Trust that the process laid out here will support you.

3. **Request space.** You may feel tempted to get straight to the resolution, but never underestimate the power of reconnecting to your own energy first. When requesting space, make sure to come to an agreement on how long you'll take and when you plan to reconvene.

4. **Take ownership for your role in the conflict.**
    Conflicts require two parties, and you can always identify something you could have done better.

While your ego will be focused on how the other person was wrong or has hurt you, find what you can own, and apologize from the heart.

Note: you should never begin with the words, "I'm sorry you feel that way." The other person's feelings are not yours to be sorry for, and that is a passive-aggressive statement. If you really feel you didn't do anything that warrants being sorry, I promise, there is still something to find remorse for that can be expressed with love. Perhaps try, "I'm sorry we're in this situation." That is passive, but not aggressive.

5. **Use the Intentionality Communication Method (found on pages 200–201).** This will help the other person to understand your side and what you are experiencing. Follow the process of introducing the situation, identifying your feelings, sharing the story you're telling yourself about the situation, asking for what you need, and offering an invitation for a path forward.

6. **Have a reunion.** Without fail, when I've followed these steps, even if I and the other person or group of people have not fully aligned with each other on each piece of the conflict, we've resolved to come back together in celebration of the growth we've made. Initiate an embrace, do a silly dance, or share an expression of appreciation to close the process.

KEY TAKEAWAYS

Behaviors for Choosing Love

- Tune in to your heart.
- Reaffirm the belief that life is happening for you, not to you.
- Forgive yourself and others.
- Know where you stand.
- Use acknowledgment as a gift.

Tools for Choosing Love

- Forgiveness and Acknowledgment
- Communication Method
- Conflict Playbook

CHAPTER 11

PRACTICING
PRESENCE

With the amount of information available to us, we're rarely ever forced to be alone with our thoughts and our feelings. While our devices are designed to keep us informed and connected, they're also designed to keep us engaged—with them. Often this comes at the expense of our relationships, leads to us easily giving in to distraction, and can ironically create a greater disconnectivity in how we communicate with others and ourselves.

The result of parasocial relationships, constant imagery in an endless feed, and our desire to always see, do, and consume more is that we've become entrenched in a culture of comparison. As we've explored in this book, it's hard not to feel that someone else is doing better than we are, or that we haven't achieved enough. It can be difficult not to compare our bodies and even our well-being to those of others. And so, often our efforts to stay connected have led to the creation of identities rooted only in comparing ourselves to someone or something beyond our control.

This chapter not only introduces behaviors and tools that will help you fight the urge to weigh up and compare; it will teach you how to sustain more prolonged periods of presence and help you redefine your relationship with yourself and the people around you.

Behaviors

See Everything as Your Teacher

Make intention-setting habitual.

Many of us have gotten in the habit of hitting the ground running as soon as we wake up in the morning. But running rudderless can often lead to days that are less than productive or fulfilling. Before you check your e-mail, head to the gym, or dive into your first to-do, identify how you want to feel and what behaviors will help you achieve that feeling consistently throughout your day. Even better, set your intention the night before so you can impress this intention on your subconscious as you fall asleep and then again when you wake up.

View every moment as an opportunity for growth.

Personal growth can happen when you least expect it. In some circumstances, being intentional can feel tedious, inefficient, or even unappealing. In these moments, I find that focusing on one thing I can learn from the experience or one thing I can do differently can help me make the incremental progress I'm looking for—especially with things like administrative tasks for work or mundane chores. By using this technique right before I start the task I've been avoiding or dreading, I empower myself to stay present. This helps me realize that every moment is an opportunity to further open my heart and expand my consciousness. You can always become a more evolved and more aware person.

Rate your intention at the end of the day.

On a scale from 1 to 10, rate how well you went with your intention throughout the day. This isn't to focus on how perfect you were. Instead, give your rating based on how often you came back to your intention to redirect your behaviors and your thoughts. There's no shame in getting derailed, as long as you identify what you can do better the next time. A simple reflection can help you from straying the next time and is another opportunity to practice self-compassion.

Quiet Your Mind

Meditate *your* way.

Meditation, much like prayer, looks and feels different for everyone. What calms you isn't necessarily calming for the next person. My favorite type of meditation is the Vipassana style of 60 minutes in silence. I know for many others this can seem daunting, so they avoid the practice all together. Get creative—you can meditate while chopping vegetables, coloring, walking in nature, or listening to chanting or binaural beats. Home in on what soothes your nervous system and what feels the most serene. Identify what will bring your mind the most peace. Seek out or create an environment that will help you feel grounded in the present moment and better able to turn inward.

Contemplate meaningful questions.

Existentialism can be an intimidating topic, but spending time to ponder deeper inquiries into our human experience can be profound. Sometimes, just asking questions can have a slanted approach—shame or judgment can taint the exercise. But that doesn't have to be the case. Even if you ask a difficult question that you may not be prepared to fully answer, that just means it's part of your unfinished business. And we all have unfinished business. That's what makes us human and what makes life worth living.

Some of the questions I've been asking myself lately include: *What kind of father do I want to be? Did my partner and I know each other in another life? Why am I hard on myself? How can I be of more service?*

Try writing down questions around topics you find the most confronting or intriguing. It may feel loud inside at first—but that's just the early chatter, the rumblings of your ruminations, and the prologue to deeper explorations of your inner world.

Initiate regular pauses.

Do you have phantom phone syndrome? Do you constantly need to see a screen or listen to a podcast to kill time on a commute? Do you find yourself doing anything and everything to avoid being alone with your thoughts? When we distract ourselves we are doing more than just avoiding our thoughts, we are also avoiding our feelings.

During my Vipassana experience, when I went 10 days without speaking or interacting with anyone, I actually didn't miss the noise. And it's not as hard as you think it might be.

It can be very challenging to be patient and sit with yourself in stillness and silence. But the benefit of getting to know yourself better by being still and being aware can raise you to the highest vibrations. We all need pauses in life, so take them when they show up, surrender, and embrace the art of doing nothing at all.

Adopt healthy rituals.

When I was at the lowest point in my life, I scribbled on a piece of paper 16 activities that would get me through the day, baby steps that just might even put a smile on my face. It's a sobering moment to be in your early 30s and have to write down the words *walking in nature* to keep you from dancing with your demons or dabbling too far in depressive behavior—but sometimes that's what accountability looks like. And in my case, it's not an exaggeration. These things really did save my life. So my advice to you is to start out even with the goal of one new healthy habit a day. Then try another, until you're regularly crafting rituals that you enjoy and that genuinely boost your body, mind, and spirit.

Be Grateful for the Present Moment

Find infinite joy in the simplest of things.

The world is an amazing place. What's more amazing? There's no one in the world exactly like you—which means that your precise experience, understanding, and observations are unique to you and you alone. Take advantage of that. Look at the sunset from where you're standing and know that you are the only person in the world to see it from that exact vantage point at that exact moment. Or savor your favorite ice cream, one lick at a time. The Danish word *hygge* embraces this notion of finding happiness in the smallest joys of life. See how you can create a little bit of hygge in each of your days.

Find ways throughout the day to share gratitude.

Gratitude is infectious, and there are many ways to practice it. A gratitude walk is simply when you walk and identify, vocally or internally, everything you're grateful for. I've started doing these almost daily with my partner and friends, and it's incredibly satisfying to hear what they're appreciative of and to riff off of our mutual gratitudes. I also really enjoy keeping a gratitude journal—one where I focus on what I'm grateful for in each of the five priorities. Try a gratitude walk with your loved ones. Keep notes on what you're thankful for in how you're able to love, grow, serve, play, and create. These simple practices will help you immediately ground into a state of presence.

Share appreciation for people in your life.

Tomorrow is never guaranteed, and regret is often the result of making the assumption that it is. There's no reason to wait to share your appreciation for someone, and it's impossible to over-appreciate others. Tell the people in your life you love them and do it often; it actually becomes contagious. If a good memory of someone pops into your head, drop them a line, call them, or even better, surprise them with an old-fashioned handwritten note. You never know how much this can brighten someone's day.

> ## Seek Internal Wisdom,
> ## Not External Validation

Trust your intuition.

Learning to trust your instincts is crucial for decision-making. Your intuition is often referred to as your "sixth sense" and is not something you learn, because it is an innate wisdom, but it is something you can learn to strengthen. Your body is the ultimate intelligence in guiding you toward what is in your best interest. Just like thoughts are the language of the mind, feelings are the language of the body. The more you are able to tune in to your body's cues, the more you will be able to identify what people, environments, and things are most compatible for you. Think of your intuition as your inner guidance system and look within for the answers you seek.

Don't define growth in material form.

Growth in a company is often defined by numbers, tangible profits, return on investment, key performance indicators, and lines on a graph. But a company is a finite entity. You are a person, not a product. During my marriage, I got distracted by measuring my growth in terms of financial well-being. I believed that being in a big house—with a lot of money, multiple businesses, and unlimited access to luxury and travel—was the sign that I had arrived. I had grown up, made something of myself, and I was really living "the life."

I got a stark reminder that none of those things had anything to do with my physical or mental health, or the health of my marriage. The only thing they provided was a false sense of security. Don't fall into the arrival fallacy trap—"When I get this, I'll be that," or "When this happens, I'll be happier." Instead, avoid focusing on what you've acquired, and explore the meaning behind what you've achieved. Also, give yourself grace. You are a work in progress at all times—meaning that your growth happens alongside all your flaws and in tandem with all your ups and downs.

Avoid suffering by seeking equilibrium within.

Suffering is a consequence of internal imbalance. Pain is unavoidable, but suffering and prolonging pain and misery is the byproduct of neglecting your inner peace. In today's world, suffering is sometimes portrayed as a virtue. As I've noted, if you suffered while building your start-up, you're written about in business headlines. You're portrayed as somehow more worthy of the fruits of your labor because your labor included suffering. And for what? Sure, you have at your coattails the great hero's story of overcoming the obstacles to reach your life's dream. But was it necessary to deprive yourself of that much sleep and sanity? At what cost was it to you—and to your family? Finding balance is not banal. It's self-preserving and self-empowering.

> ## Choose Whom You Surround Yourself With

Invest in strong support systems.

I rely on my entrepreneurial and community groups, my mentors, and my friends in more ways than I can count. And I reciprocate that same support for them. It's worth it—and sometimes just knowing they are there is enough. The hard truth is that sometimes you need someone else to help you get out of your own way. These people can be your lifeline in difficult times. One phone call at a critical juncture can stop you from spiraling into further negative belief loops.

Define what you want out of your relationships.

This can be one of the most effective ways to positively shape your relationships. What I look for in my close connections are characteristics in others that will help me become a better version of myself. I want people who can be fully open, who reciprocate the energy I give to them back to me, and who share my values. I find that life is more playful and satisfying when shared.

Do a regular analysis of whom you bring into your life—and especially those you bring into your inner temple. Inner-temple people should fulfill the characteristics that are most important to you. Take an inventory of the different people in your life, define the importance and meaning they hold for you, and make sure to nurture your inner-temple relationships regularly.

Spend the majority of your time with high-vibrational people.

I always admired my partner's late mother, because she would enter any situation as the most curious person in the room and find a way to make anyone she met laugh and feel important. Her ability to see the positive in any given circumstance was extraordinary, and it was a trait that made her energy infectious. Fill your life with people who inspire you and energize you. To identify them, try asking yourself, *Does this person have positive things happening in their life? Does this person ask me and others questions? Does this person's presence make me feel buoyant and vibrant?*

Tools

Daily Reflection

This is an activity to do at the end of each day to shine light on the positive things in your life. It's a great way to identify your desired feelings, express your gratitude, and reflect on what you've learned. This is also an easy way to habituate the recoding process by reinforcing positive belief loops.

You can journal your responses or answer these questions aloud around the dinner table with your loved ones—kids love answering these questions too!

1. What was your favorite moment of the
    day, and why?

2. What are you most grateful for, and why?

3. How well did you align with your daily intention?
    (Use a rating from 1 to 10 and then dig deeper
    with these follow-up questions: What did you
    learn? What would you do differently if you had
    the chance?)

4. What do you appreciate about yourself, and why?
    (Or if you're in a group, what do you appreciate
    about someone else, and why?)

16 Lifesavers

I call these Lifesavers, but put simply, they're 16 small steps you
can take on your path to Intentionality. When you're feeling low,
stuck, or lost in life, actions from this list will bring you back to
the present moment with things guaranteed to raise your energy
and vibration. Start by trying to check off at least three of these
activities each day. Feel proud of yourself on the days you do and
compassionate on the days you don't. Note that this list is just to
start from and inspire you. Once you get the hang of it, custom-
ize one that works best for you.

1. **Journal.** Spend eight minutes and 20 seconds letting
    your thoughts flow. This is the amount of time it
    takes sunlight to reach Earth, and metaphorically for
    your subconscious to shed light on what you need to
    pay attention to. I highly recommend putting pen
    to paper instead of using a digital device, as you'll be
    more connected to your internal processing.

2. **Practice gratitude.** Write down something you're grateful for in each of the life priorities: love, grow, serve, play, and create. Describe what you're grateful for and why. Reflect on how these people or things made you feel, and how you can bring more of them into your life.

3. **Meditate.** Dedicate time to quiet the mind and body and go inward. Try not to be hard on yourself about what being a "good meditator" looks like. It's more important that you get into the rhythm rather than doing it the way you think you're "supposed to"— remember that it's called a "practice" for a reason. There's no one right way.

4. **Do yin yoga or qigong.** These forms of light movement are inspired by the art of effortless power and will help you calm your mind and relax into your body. Try your best to keep your focus on body sensations and the breath and focus your intention on moving energy throughout your body.

5. **Breathe.** There are a variety of breathwork techniques you can use that range in length of time, style, and intensity. Conscious breathing will reset your system no matter the circumstance. You can find a variety of my guided breathwork sessions on the "Intentionality" app, available in Google Play and Apple stores.

6. **Pray.** You can write your own prayer or use one from whatever text inspires you. Use "I am" statements to reinforce your positive belief loops—but remember, you must also align your behaviors to really give these statements power. Take time to recite your prayer each morning and night, preferably when you're in an alpha or theta state.

7. **Practice grounding.** Bury your toes in the sand.
    Walk barefoot on the forest floor. Lie down in a park.
    When possible, try to be in direct connection with
    Mother Earth, and let her take away your negative
    energy and nurture you with unconditional love.

8. **Embrace the sun.** Let the rays envelop you in their
    warmth, melting away any negativity it encounters.
    Even as little as 10 minutes of exposure will boost
    your whole-body health—and especially your mood.

9. **Go for a walk.** Take a stroll around the block.
    Explore a new neighborhood or park. Meet a friend
    for a "walk and talk." Let this be a mindful and
    leisurely activity rather than a challenging hike or
    faster-paced walk, and it's always better to go outside
    when possible.

10. **Eat a healthy snack or meal.** It's common to turn
    to food to numb our feelings. As tempting as that
    might seem, choose the opposite. Be intentional
    about making food that will nourish you and eat
    it consciously, not zoned out while watching TV or
    scrolling your phone.

11. **Sleep well.** When you're struggling and stressed,
    your body needs extra sleep. Make sure to allot
    more time for sleep than normal. In addition, treat
    yourself to a little nap during the day.

12. **Exercise.** When you exercise, your body releases
    endorphins that trigger positive feelings in your
    body and your mind. Use the challenge of a workout
    to physically change your state of being, and your
    mind will follow.

13. **Do something fun.** Allow yourself to indulge
    in something that brings you joy. Jump on a
    trampoline, pick up that old Hula-Hoop, go to the
    movies, etc. Allow yourself to reignite your childlike
    play and wonder, and lose yourself in the act.

14. **Hygge Plan time.** Hygge comes from Danish culture and is anything that brings about the qualities of comfort and coziness and creates an environment of well-being. Make a cup of your favorite tea, light some candles, run yourself a bath, dive into a good book—the simple things in life can often lead to the most pleasure.

15. **Do something kind.** Mahatma Gandhi said, "The best way to find yourself is to lose yourself in the service of others." Find somewhere you can volunteer for the day. Call a friend to let them know you're thinking about them. Be extra friendly to the grocery-store clerk. Your acts of kindness will not only help others, but leave you feeling good too.

16. **Work on your craft.** Get creative and do whatever it is that lights you up. This might be working on enhancing the skills of your current career, doing that hobby you never seem to have time for, or exploring a newfound passion.

Gratitude Exercise

Set a timer for 15 minutes, and write down in detail all the things you're grateful for in your life. Use descriptive language and tap into your feelings by explaining why you're grateful. You can use these prompts and categories to get the ball rolling:

I'm grateful for _____ because I can _____ .

I appreciate _____ because it/he/she/they make(s)

me feel _____ .

I feel fortunate to have _____ because it allows

me to _____ .

Categories: animals/pets, career, education, family, friends, health, home, lover, money, nature, technology, travel

KEY TAKEAWAYS

Behaviors for Practicing Presence

- See everything as your teacher.
- Quiet your mind.
- Be grateful for the present moment.
- Seek internal wisdom, not external validation.
- Choose whom you surround yourself with.

Tools for Practicing Presence

- Daily Reflection
- 16 Lifesavers
- Gratitude Exercise

CHAPTER 12

PRIORITIZING FEELINGS

In a results-driven world, one that often measures success only through the lens of what happens at the finish line, it's easy to lose sight of the emotional experiences we have along the way. But throughout my career and my relationships, I've found that when I was able to refrain from living too far into the future, from placing my mind at the finish line of a project or situation, I was able to process the intermittent feelings that were impacting me in real time.

This chapter helps you focus on the behaviors and tools that provide real-time data to inform how you're evolving during the full arc of your personal experiences. It will underscore the significance of this intention—that thinking less about the long run and feeling more into the moment at hand yields greater, lasting change.

Behaviors

Become Aware of Your Feelings

Identify the sensations in your body.

Notice where you feel tension or tingling—where you might be feeling numbness or sensations of any type. Ask yourself what feeling is connected to this sensation. As I've previously mentioned, thoughts are the language of the mind and emotions are the language of the body. Connecting your physical sensations to your feelings can help you gain greater insights into what your body is trying to tell you.

Have a regular journaling practice.

You're not always going to have awareness of all the things that may be contributing to how you are feeling in the moment. But you have the opportunity to explore your triggers, and to identify ways to navigate these moments better in the future.

I like to journal in the morning to set my intention and express my gratitude. And I like to write about what I'm visioning or what I'm creating. I also love to map out a positive belief loop and connect it with the behaviors that will support my desired feelings. At the end of the day, I often reflect on how my day went, how my negative and positive belief loops may have been activated, and what I need to work on.

One thing you may find very helpful with journaling is to create daily prompts for yourself, such as "What's a challenging conversation I need to have?" or "What's a difficult decision I need to make?" These can really help you get clarity in areas where you may be stuck and determine what the next necessary steps are.

Discover your Love Story.

We all have deeply embedded belief loops around love. As we get older, we accumulate stories, wounds, and even trauma from prior relationships. These things color our perspective and the lens through which we view love. For years, I did not think I deserved the kind of love I have in my relationship now. I did not know then what I know now, and that's because I was unaware that the picture I had painted in my head of long-term relationships was deeply shrouded by the toxicity of my parents' relationship. Once I was able to cultivate the positive feelings that nourish a healthy relationship, I opened up new ways of showing love to others and to myself that I never knew were possible. Your Love Story helps you understand what formed your beliefs about love and how they might be affecting your current relationships. Think about how your parents demonstrated love and what sayings you heard about love growing up. When you were young, how did you imagine your intimate love partnership would look? How similar is that outlook to your current reality?

Take Ownership of Your Feelings

Release any blame or projections.

Unfortunately, blame, shame, and defensiveness have become methods of survival in today's society. But they are egoic drivers and do not serve you in any way. Interrogate yourself. What blame or projections have come about as a result of your negative feelings? How did blame and projection create a disservice to you and those around you? Discover ways to recognize and counteract those pesky and counterproductive behaviors. Once you understand the casualties of anger and accusations and choose accountability, you'll find new levels of inner peace.

Apologize when you've gone off course.

No one is perfect. We have all paved destructive paths at one point or another. It's important to acknowledge those we've hurt in the process and apologize for that behavior. The problem with unowned actions is that they create an environment of stagnancy. They foster resentment between people. One of the most powerful phrases in the English language is, "I'm sorry." And that's because when you acknowledge your missteps and apologize, you not only show humility and humanity, but you show that you have agency over yourself and your feelings, and that you're capable of understanding the profound impact you can have on others.

Let go of owning others' feelings.

Do your actions have consequences? Yes. Can they impact the emotional state of others? Of course. But feelings are personal. For example, if I do something that results in you feeling hurt, the language around this situation matters. I did something you found hurtful. You are hurting. I may have feelings of regret or disappointment in myself, but I cannot own your feelings because if I do, I'm assisting you in losing agency over your emotions in a situation where I've already likely lost your trust.

It's critical that you understand, and continue to remind yourself, that you're not responsible for the feelings of others. That we are is a fallacy that when adopted, even with good intentions, does not end well. Even if you've played a role in how someone else feels, remember that you are not physically feeling their feelings. Take ownership of your feelings and acknowledge the feelings of others. But draw the line there so you avoid the temptation to take their feelings on as your own. Avoiding this will ensure you don't undermine their experience and rob them of the opportunity to move through difficult emotions at their own pace and in their own way.

> Live in Alignment with
> Your Desired Feelings

Identify your desired feelings.

I like to do this specifically for the different areas of my life—my intimate relationships, my career, and my well-being. I pick three desired feelings to help anchor me to my goals from a feelings-first approach. I then use these desired feelings to help me make my decisions. These can be decisions about projects I undertake, the structure of my life, how much work I should take on, how many vacations I can set aside, and so on.

For example, with my partner, I want to feel peaceful, playful, and connected. So whenever I'm triggered by a negative belief loop, I take a moment to ask myself, *Is this behavior going to lead me to feel those desired feelings?* Explore the different areas of your life with this tool and ask yourself, *What are the three top feelings I desire to have?* Naming your desired feelings will bring a much-needed compass to how you pursue and preserve what matters to you.

Envision your ideal feeling state.

The future can be a dangerous place to live when you attempt to move yourself too far ahead and therefore pull yourself out of the present. However, it can be helpful to visualize yourself in an ideal feeling state.

When I have a presentation to give, I don't spend a great deal of time considering what will happen after I speak: I avoid the traditional musings such as, *Will people talk about it? Will they post about it? How can I make sure I get hired to come speak again?* Instead, I focus on the positive feelings I want to evoke in the audience, the feeling I want to leave them with by the end of the talk, and the feeling I hope to have at the close of my remarks. When possible, try putting your future in the context of feeling—of how you would ideally like to feel in the minutes, hours, days, weeks, months, and years ahead. That way, you'll be better able to examine the necessary interim behaviors that you must prioritize today. In other words, when you envision your future from the lens of feelings, you'll keep yourself from putting the cart before the horse and going straight off the cliff.

Regularly reflect on your behavior.

You can be your own worst enemy, especially when it comes to steady progress. Consider how your behavior either contributes to or detracts from your desired feelings. You can track this by writing down your behaviors and seeing if they fit into negative or positive belief loops. This will help you have an honest inner dialogue about what is serving or undercutting your headway.

Respond Rather than React

Prepare yourself for challenging interactions.

While you don't want to negatively presume what another person will say during an encounter (and similarly, you don't want to harbor too many expectations of a kumbaya moment), you can, as they say, "keep your side of the street clean." Write down, say aloud, or role-play with someone else the points you hope to get across. Focus on how you can stay in your body and avoid being triggered into activating your negative belief loops. This is irrespective of the other person's behavior and should be rooted in you being able to honor and acknowledge your role in the situation. Preparing yourself will help you take the edge off and respond intentionally when the time comes for the real interaction.

Distinguish being right from being happy.

Conversations with conflict can escalate quickly. We've been conditioned to operate under the illusion that being right will make us happy—but what if you could respond and honor your desired feelings rather than react and regret it later? Try taking a full breath in and a full breath out, pausing for five seconds before responding, and asking yourself, "Do I want to be right, or do I want to be happy?"

Connect your desired feelings with a corresponding behavior.

By now, you know the architecture of belief loops—which means that you know your behaviors directly correspond with your feelings. And you may also know by now that making these corresponding connections often requires you to question your choices. Yes—question the choices you make while you're making them, and ask yourself if your choice will lead to your desired feelings. Ask if the behavior you're leaning in to is helping or hurting your ability to feel and function at your very best. It's a pretty simple filter, but reject whatever doesn't meet this criterion. One of the most important things to remember is that you won't be able to connect a desired feeling with a behavior until you've clearly identified the feeling. Be sure to take that first step before connecting further dots.

Use curiosity, not conflict.

Conflict can often drag on much longer than is needed when we don't take the time to consider each other's experiences. My partner and I have been preparing to have a baby. Recently, I was talking about how excited I am about the process, and I felt deflated when she looked sad and distant every time I brought it up. In my mind, this was supposed to be a positive experience for both of us, so what was going on with her? After a disagreement, we employed the Conflict Playbook and took some space from each other for the first half of the day. I then invited her to join me in a cacao ceremony—I told her my intention was to listen, hold the space and stay in my masculine, and be curious about everything that might be coming up for her. By staying silent, I was able to allow her to release it all. I learned that she was going through the anticipatory grief of learning she was pregnant and not being able to share that moment with her late mother. She then asked me questions—and we discovered that we both had coded beliefs around the birthing process that hadn't yet been addressed. Suddenly we were connected and not in conflict. Be curious about the other's experience instead of resorting to conjecture or combativeness. Listen. Ask. Engage.

Be in a High-Vibrational State

Clear your emotions.

Emotions that aren't cleared become stagnant energy in your system and can continue to attract negative circumstances to you. The breath can be a proactive measure to stop yourself from short-circuiting and help with clearing your emotions throughout the day. One of the reasons that the breath is so powerful is because it is always available to you, wherever you are. It's the quickest, most efficient tool at your disposal—which is why it's so easy and so important to make a habit out of intentionally using it.

Be the example.

You don't have to project your views or tell each and every detail of your personal growth journey. When you're in a high-vibrational state, people will be magnetized to you whether you're speaking or not. Very often, the most wisdom comes through actions and not words. Focus less on providing explanations and more on being the example. When you live with intention, and when you maintain it with supportive behaviors, you'll see and feel a noticeable difference. After all, you're a part of the great awakening and the universal shift in consciousness—own it.

Find a safe space for reflection.

Introspection doesn't always have to be a solo act, and Intentionality doesn't have to be a path you pave alone. Consider where and with whom you feel the most able to be yourself. Find a therapist, coach, or emotional support group with whom you feel safe to share reflections and explore your inner world. Knowing you have others for feedback or just a friendly ear can make your darkest hours a bit lighter.

Tools

Love Story

Your Love Story (formed by your belief loops around love) is the lens through which you view your life and influences everything in it, because life is ultimately about how we love. That's why an awareness of your Love Story is so critical and will be the major catalyst for developing healthier relationships with yourself and others.

Discover your Love Story by engaging with the following prompts:

1. Revisit your childhood.

Reflect on your childhood and upbringing, discover how your early years shaped your current beliefs about love and relationships.

What's your earliest memory of experiencing love?

How did love impact and shape your childhood?

How were feelings of love expressed in your childhood home?

What were the sayings you heard about love and relationships? For example, "I love you because you're so smart," or "Marriage isn't about love; it's about compromise."

What did your parents teach you about love and relationships?

2. Unlock your love timeline.

Starting from birth to five years of age and moving forward in five-year increments (6 to 10, 11 to 15, 16 to 20, etc.), write down any impactful events or memories you have.

Try to capture both the positive and negative memories you have around love and relationships, listing any key events that dramatically transformed your life. For example, divorce, infidelity, death, and so on. For each of these memories and events, explore how your beliefs, thoughts, behaviors, and feelings about love and relationships were impacted.

3. Write your current Love Story.

Explore your current thoughts, behaviors, and feelings about love and relationships. Tap into your present experience and be honest about how you currently think and behave—avoid the temptation to sugarcoat your reality. If you're not currently in an intimate relationship, write about your most recent experience.

These are the thoughts I have around love and relationships:

How I behave in my relationship is:

How my relationship makes me feel is:

4. Reflect on how your Love Story is impacting your life.

Take a moment to reflect on how everything leading up to now has impacted how you show up in your relationships. Try to identify some of the core beliefs you have around love. Do you feel safe, do you feel valued, or do you feel unworthy, or that you're a disappointment? Then identify some ways you can enhance your positive belief loops around love and eliminate the negative. And finally, commit to one step you can take today—remembering that Intentionality is all about incremental steps on your path forward.

The beliefs I have around love and my relationship are:

My Love Story has impacted my life in the following ways:

What I like about my Love Story:

What I want to change about my Love Story:

One way I commit to making change today:

Extraordinary Day

Think about a day in the future, and imagine your ideal life—the way it would be without any limitations, where anything is possible. Who would be a part of your day? What activities would you do? What would you feel like?

Set a timer for 15 minutes and engage in stream-of-consciousness writing. This is where you let your creative thoughts flow through you without inhibition, doing your best not to lift your pen from the paper. While writing, do not worry about grammar or punctuation. Simply focus on describing all that you are imagining in as much detail as possible. Identify the feelings that coincide with those visions in an expressive way.

After you complete the exercise, reflect on these questions:

What feelings repeatedly came up in my descriptions?

How did this exercise motivate or inspire me?

Does this day seem achievable immediately or in the near future? If not, what can I do to change that?

Desired Feelings

Your desired feelings are what will bring you the most fulfillment and satisfaction in your life. I recommend identifying three desired feelings to use as a benchmark and tuning in to these feelings daily. The following prompts will help you identify your desired feelings—you can do this for your life in general or direct it toward a specific area, such as your relationship, career, well-being, etc.

1. Using a rating from 1 to 10, how well do you think you're flourishing in all areas of your life?

2. What are three negative feelings preventing you from giving a 10 to any area?

3. What are three factors that could be contributing to your negative feelings?

4. What are the top three positive feelings that would make you feel like you're flourishing in your life and give you a rating of 10?

5. What are three priorities in the short term (immediate) and the long term (one year) that will lead you to feel more of these positive feelings?

KEY TAKEAWAYS

Behaviors for Prioritizing Feelings

- Become aware of your feelings.
- Take ownership of your feelings.
- Live in alignment with your desired feelings.
- Respond rather than react.
- Be in a high-vibrational state.

Tools for Prioritizing Feelings

- Love Story
- Extraordinary Day
- Desired Feelings

Part V

SCIENTIFIC MANIFESTATION

If you will assume your desire and live there as though it were true, no power on earth can stop it from becoming a fact.

— **NEVILLE GODDARD**

Manifestation has a reputation for being "airy-fairy," but there's a science to it—literally. While I may refer to it as a miracle or anyone practicing it as a miracle worker, manifestation is not make-believe. In fact, the whole concept of manifestation is *scientific*.

Did you know that world-renowned scientist and theoretical physicist Albert Einstein famously once said, "Everything is energy. Match the frequency of the reality you want and you cannot help but get that reality. It can be no other way. This is not philosophy. This is physics."?

Let's consider the formulas you learned in basic physics and its law of cause and effect—which essentially shows that if you have one, you have the other. Let's take water, for example. When you have water, this also means you have the ability to create ice. And of course, when you have ice, you have the ability to melt it into water. You also may have learned that when you have electricity, you can have magnetism, and vice versa. Electricity and magnetism are essentially two aspects of the same thing. When you change an electric field, it creates a magnetic field, and when you change a magnetic field, it creates an electric field. This is what we're doing with scientific manifestation. We're creating a strong field to magnetize our creation toward us.

Put all this in the context of Intentionality, and what it ultimately means is this: If you have the feelings, then you must eventually have the outcomes. And the distance between these two is where the process of scientific manifestation comes in.

But the thing is—a miracle doesn't just happen on its own. It requires a miracle worker. What you've learned up until now has you primed for this role. First, you learned what makes up your system. Then you learned how coding from the external world has shaped your identity and your belief loops—and you were introduced to repetition and energy interventions, two pivotal methods for recoding.

So why is it so important for you to have learned these lessons first? Well, scientific manifestation isn't really an effective process unless you've already done the personal growth work and preparation that comes with repetition and energy interventions. The intent of scientific manifestation is to accelerate and align the desires of your conscious mind with your subconscious beliefs and the infinite intelligence of the Universal Mind. But here's the tricky part—you manifest from your subconscious. If you have negative belief loops running and you try to manifest, you may actually attract the opposite of what you want. So if you create your positive belief loops first, you can then use this information to rapidly accelerate the desired intentions in your life.

Everything that is manifested into form begins in unmanifested form. Everything is a mental projection: Whatever you desire already exists in the Universal Mind. The scientific manifestation process is a proven formula that creates your desired reality through a shift in your state of consciousness and empowers you to do less, allow more, and make a quantum leap in your Intentionality journey. And if you follow it, it *will* work! All it requires is a positive belief loop, tapping into the energy of the Universal Mind, and living as though you've already made your miracle—because you have.

CHAPTER 13

THE THREE C's

Throughout this book, I've pointed out that there are masculine and feminine energies within each of us—and I've highlighted how the "doing" energy of the masculine and the "being" energy of the feminine are necessary components in our system. But what is also important about understanding the existence and balance of these energies is that when harnessed effectively, they will be critical ingredients of the scientific manifestation process.

The three steps in this process are *clarify*, *conceive*, and *claim*. One way to help understand this is to consider the process of making a baby. For the purposes of this example, I'm referring to a planned, cisgendered, heterosexual conception without complications. Of course, there are many different paths and ways to create your family, and each reflects scientific manifestation in nuanced ways.

During the *clarify* step, people discuss the details of the optimal time for impregnation, how they're going to do it, and how they're going to afford it. This is our conscious mind and our more masculine energy in the situation coming into play.

The second step is to *conceive*. This is when the masculine must come together with the feminine for impregnation—and in context of the minds, when the conscious penetrates the subconscious.

And the third step is to *claim*. There's no material evidence immediately after intercourse that a baby has been created. But once conception is confirmed, there's a nine-month process of claiming the baby, of believing in its creation, and supporting and nurturing it. And throughout this period is when the subconscious and conscious, the feminine and masculine, vibe in concert with one another led by the feminine energy of intuition and nurturance—when the conscious fully listens to the guidance and insight of the subconscious all the way through to the manifestation of the baby at birth.

When we apply these three *C*'s to our own experiences, we can think of it much the same way. First, when we *clarify* our intention, we are stirring our conscious mind and our masculine energy. When we *conceive* the intention, our masculine and feminine energies, our conscious and subconscious, come together in synchronicity. Our subconscious instigates the powers of love and gratitude to tap into and connect deeply with the Universal Mind. This seeds our manifestation. Of course, the seeds then need nourishment and the alignment of all our energies. At this stage, we need to deter bad energy and negativity and shepherd our positive feelings intentionally and all the way through to *claiming* our manifestation.

When you implement the three *C*'s, you must get really clear on the feelings you desire, believe that whatever you are manifesting is possible, and transition that belief into a reality.

Clarify

This first part of the process happens while you are still in the conscious mind. It requires clarifying your desired feelings and your desired outcome, and then creating a movie scene that represents this evolution.

1. Clearly define exactly what you want to create in your life.

There are a few things to note here:

It's important to be specific. Instead of saying you want a house, be really specific about where the house is, what kind of lighting it gets, how many bedrooms and bathrooms it has, the aesthetics of it, what surrounds the house, etc.

It's important that you believe that it can happen. I'm a 38-year-old, five-foot-nine-inch Australian who grew up in the countryside of Tasmania and never played basketball growing up. Saying that I'd like to be an NBA all-star doesn't align with some of the realities at this point in my life. However, I could come to terms with other ideas, like managing a basketball team. Use logic (but be aware that there is a fine line for not succumbing to negative belief loops) to make sure your manifestation is achievable.

Do not allow yourself to go into reasons why what you want can't happen. We've been conditioned to have limiting beliefs, so it's natural that they'll come up. If you find this happening, simply come back to the details of your manifestation and don't indulge the negative thoughts.

2. Clearly define three to five feelings that you will feel when you achieve your outcome.

We've talked a lot about the importance of identifying your desired feelings, and you've even walked through a few exercises to help you get in touch with what yours might be. Remember—you want a desired outcome because you believe it will give you particular feelings. Here are some common desired feelings to inspire you: free, excited, in awe, abundant, inspired, proud, peaceful, playful, expansive, confident, grounded.

3. Create a short movie scene that you'll play on repeat in your mind.

Think of this as playing a movie in your mind where you are the key actor and the scene plays out with you behaving in the ways that will lead to your desired feelings.

Here are some prompts to help you create this one scene. Remember, it should be short and succinct.

- What is something that would likely occur after you've already achieved your desired outcome? For example, if you're trying to attract a partner, it could be introducing your partner to your parents. If this were to occur, then it means that you must have already found your partner.

- What would each of your senses be doing in this scene? Go into detail to ensure that the scene you picture evokes joy and fulfillment: things like a big smile, clapping your hands, closing your eyes in a moment of gratitude, etc.

- What is the short sentence you would say that exemplifies the manifestation is complete? It could be something like "How wonderful, I did it!" Or it could be "Document has been signed!" or "I'm going to be a dad!"

Conceive

The next part of the process is best done right before going to bed at night, or in the first stages of waking in the morning when you can more easily access the theta state. In this step, the conscious mind is going to be imprinting on the subconscious mind. But first, you have to get connected to the higher power, the Universal Mind.

1. Drop into a meditative state.

Use your breath to slow down your brain waves from beta to alpha and eventually to theta. This is where the conscious mind is nearly turned off. We need to be in this state so that our limiting beliefs cannot influence our creation.

2. Expand your consciousness.

To access a high-vibrational state, get into your heart center and start bringing forward the highest positive feelings of love, appreciation, and gratitude. Connect to your higher self and the unlimited power you have within.

3. Play your movie.

As soon as you reach theta, the drowsy state just before you fall asleep or right when you wake up, have the conscious mind press play on the movie scene that you created in the *clarify* stage. Actually live out the movie scene rather than just watch it. Do this by bringing all of your senses alive and repeating the scene over and over again until you feel that the creation has occurred, or you fall asleep.

It's important to imagine yourself already doing and having what you want to experience. When you imagine something in the present moment, it's instantaneously created in the quantum world and will, in time, materialize in the physical plane.

Claim

The final step of the process is to *claim* your manifestation. At this stage the subconscious and conscious mind are communicating back and forth with one another.

1. Live in gratitude.

When either you wake up or come out of your theta meditation, give thanks that the creation has happened. This can be expressed out loud or silently within.

2. Align with the creation.

Choose to focus your awareness on thoughts and behaviors that align with the fact that you've created your desired outcome. Ignore any evidence in conflict with your manifestation. There may be some leftover residue from previous subconscious beliefs, but if you don't pay them any attention, they won't come into your intention.

- Speak confidently that you are already who you want to be and have what you desire. Use "I am" statements to solidify this, such as "I am healthy, I am wealthy, I am happy."

- Think about how you would behave, knowing that the creation has occurred. Act as if it has already happened, because it has.

3. Take action on insights.

The subconscious and Universal Mind will create a plan for how you will achieve your desired outcome and communicate the required steps to your conscious mind.

- Be in receivership of the insights.

- Take action on the insights that you receive.

- Stay in balance. Be at peace.

- Don't be attached to how the creation will play out.

- Don't try to control things or force an outcome.

4. Revise any actions that are not in alignment with your desired outcome.

At the end of each day, identify any behaviors that were out of alignment with your manifestation. Imagine yourself redoing the moment with a behavior that is more aligned with your desired outcome.

To best initially explore what this process can do for you, here's a circuit breaker to use to kick-start the scientific manifestation process. This Theta Breath will help you get out of your thinking mind and be more able to imprint on your subconscious. Once you've mapped out your manifestation with the three C's, use this exercise to access the feelings you identified and to start to conceive the movie you've created. Remember—as soon as you feel a shift in consciousness, this is your sign that the manifestation is complete.

Circuit Breaker:
The Theta Breath

In this breath, you're priming your subconscious mind to create your desires by co-creating with the Universal Mind. This is a downregulated breath that puts you into a theta state—the slow brain wave state between waking and sleep where your subconscious mind is most suggestible.

You will be breathing to the rhythm of 4-8-16-4—inhaling through your nose for a count of 4, holding for a count of 8, exhaling out your mouth for a count of 16, and holding for a count of 4. In this breath, you'll be awakening your third eye and activating your sixth chakra.

Step One: *Sit in a chair or on the ground, get comfortable, and close your eyes. Press your lips together, resting your tongue lightly on the roof of your mouth.*

As you prepare for the breath, identify something that you wish to manifest. Ask yourself, *How would I see myself if I achieved my desire? What feelings would I feel? When is a time that I've felt these feelings before?*

Step Two: *Breathe in through your nose for four counts.*

As you breathe in, invite the infinite power and love of the Universal Mind into your heart.

Step Three: *Hold your breath for a count of eight.*

As you hold your breath, feel the energy building.

Step Four: *Exhale through your mouth for a count of 16 while looking up to your third eye.*

Feel the power of infinite love emanating slowly and powerfully outward.

Step Five: *Hold on the exhale for a count of four.*

Feel the expansiveness and openness as you connect to your higher self and the Universal Mind.

Step Six: *Repeat Steps Two through Five as you follow the directive below.*

Focus your attention on the feelings that you identified in Step One and really feel them. Run a scene in your mind that shows you in this state, where the desire is already achieved. Play it like a movie in your mind and imagine that you're actually living that scene in the here and now. Make the mental shift, feeling yourself taking action. You must participate in the imaginary action so that the sensations are real to you. Once you notice a feeling of relief, you can return to a normal breathing pattern and trust that your manifestation is done.

Step Seven: *Relax with the knowledge that you are already the person you would like to be and that your manifestation will come to fruition.*

Embrace the peacefulness in this deeply relaxed state.

KEY TAKEAWAYS

- The scientific manifestation process is a proven formula that creates your desired reality through a shift in your state of consciousness.

  Step 1: Clarify your desired outcome and your desired feelings using the directness associated with masculine energy.

  Step 2: Conceive—this is where the conscious mind imprints on the subconscious mind and the masculine energy penetrates the feminine energy.

  Step 3: Claim your manifestation as your reality. The subconscious and conscious mind are working together guided by the intuitive power of the feminine energy.

- Think of a time when you manifested something without having the conscious awareness of what you were doing. This is a time when you imagined a desired outcome—maybe you verbalized it to someone or just thought about it in your head—and it just happened. Walk this example through the steps of the scientific manifestation process and see how you subconsciously participated in some version of each of the steps to make it happen.

CHAPTER 14

MY MIRACLES

When I say that scientific manifestation is an accelerant for your intentions and a proven process, I'm saying that from firsthand experience. Here are some personal stories of how I've managed to become my own miracle maker.

My First Manifestation

Following the incident on my 10th birthday, I effectively stopped acknowledging or speaking to my father. Let's recap. After knowingly scheduling a commitment—a musical festival for him and many of his friends, as well as a slew of strangers—on the one day of the year we were going to spend as a family, my father became enraged that the rain was going to destroy the event he'd organized. I was old enough to feel dismissed not only by the fact that he'd scheduled the festival on my birthday, but also to feel that even when it was collapsing, his emotions were all about him—what had been done to *him*, how the weather had destroyed *his* plan, what bad luck *he* had. When I appeared in my parents' room that morning, instead of wishing me a happy birthday, he turned and without hesitation, yelled at me, "Fuck off!" On its own, when viewed in a vacuum, this could have been an anomaly. But to say that, or to say that this was my father's first real offense, would be to overlook years of prolonged physical and mental abuse, of constant fighting between my parents, and of pent-up rage between my father and me.

And so often growing up, it wasn't just rage that I was feeling. It was fear. In fact, I'd felt so much fear that when I could no longer manage the relentlessness of it, I would flee to my favorite tree—where I would hide until I felt it was safe to return to the house. One day when I was 12, after hours of terror following another one of my father's alcohol-induced outbursts, I had an out-of-body experience. I climbed the tree and I was saying to myself over and over, "I want it to be over. I want it to be over."

I believe that in this moment, my subconscious took control. I effectively went into a trance state—one where I was semiconscious and could observe what was happening but where I didn't feel I had much control. I was keenly aware that the only time my parents were able to come together and show me love was when something was medically wrong with me. I understood I needed to get them to worry, so that's what I did. Eventually they found me at the bottom of the tree, and I started shaking to get them worried that I was having a seizure. In this semiconscious state, I thought I was faking it and could snap out of it at any time. But nine hours later, I woke up in a hospital bed to discover that I'd been in a coma for the entire time.

They had tried countless ways to get a response from me but couldn't. I was confused by learning that I'd been out for nine hours. I thought, *If I was faking it, how could I fake it this well?*

So there we all were, my parents on their best behavior—and a few moments of familial unity. The doctors diagnosed me with epilepsy, and I started having more seizures.

Soon after the original incident, I went to an epilepsy ward and spent two weeks hooked up to electrodes for observation while doctors tried to induce seizures through sleep deprivation. I was sent home and put on a medication that made me lose a lot of my natural energy—and for a brief period of time, there was less rage directed at me. Life felt better. That is, until my condition became old news and the patterns set in again.

After a few weeks, my father's drunken, manic episodes started up again. I felt sad, low, and alone. I hated the feeling of the medication and the stigma of being epileptic. I reflected back to the moment when I was in that tree and realized that if I had created the epilepsy, then surely I must be able to get rid of it too. I got myself back into that trance state, saying to myself over and over again, "I am healthy. I am healthy." I visualized myself being off the medicine and not having any seizures. It was extremely emotional, and I fell asleep crying.

The next day when I got my medicine, I didn't say anything to my parents and threw it in the trash. I knew in my heart I didn't have epilepsy—and I never had a seizure again.

Unfortunately the program of injuring myself to seek attention was now coded deep inside of me. Pretty much every year of my school life, and even as an officer in the Australian Army, I would incur a significant injury. I've had two shoulder reconstructions, two ankle reconstructions, thumb surgery, wrist surgery, hand surgery, and neck surgery. Basically if surgery was an option, I would take it. It wasn't until my ex-wife brought this to my attention that I realized I might have a problem.

This led me down a path of exploring both the negative and positive manifestation powers of the mind. This is, of course, a path of self-exploration that continues today. Over the years, one of the biggest lessons I've garnered and that I carry with me is that I have the power to both hurt and heal myself. I remind myself that the law of cause and effect does not guarantee a positive outcome. It simply guarantees that when presented with a fork in the road, I have a choice to make. As the miracle maker, I can remember being in the tree and the fact that I can either accelerate or sabotage the process. And I remember that if I can manifest pain, then I can manifest healing as well when I activate the innate healing power within me.

The Great Break

In October 2020, I was in Moab, Utah, on my last mountain-bike ride of the year. I had a bit of concern about riding because it was just before the beginning of ski season. For context, everyone has a nonnegotiable—that number-one priority and passion that trumps all else. Skiing is my nonnegotiable. I simply love it. And while I wanted to bike, I also worried about the risk of injuring myself on my last ride and putting my ski season in jeopardy. I kept making this a point to my friends, saying that I didn't want to go too hard and that I would stay behind them. My partner also said something that morning, something that she'd never said before in any of my adventures: "Please be safe." Looking back, it was easy to see that we were intuitively picking up on some signs that maybe this was a day to stay in. Unfortunately, I broke my cardinal rule. I ignored my intuition. I ignored the signs and went for the ride anyway.

Eight hours later, I was in the middle of the desert with a very badly broken collarbone. I had to walk six miles in my bike cleats over treacherous terrain with an imminent sundown and the looming potential for hypothermia creeping in. Once I got to the car, I still had a three-hour drive to get to an urgent care that was open at this hour of the night.

After the X-rays confirmed the break, I saw a world-class surgeon who strongly recommended I get surgery. In fact, he shared that it would be required for me to heal properly. This was a decisive moment for me. Did I really believe in what I could do with my mind? My conditioned program was to get the surgery, as this was familiar to me. I knew how to play the victim. After all, I'd done it at least eight times in the past 10 years. However, I was a different person now. This was my moment of truth.

Against the surgeon's wishes, I declined surgery and focused on an intensive program of holistic care and self-healing. I used a variety of natural herbs, balms, and tinctures. I ate a clean diet and did strengthening exercises. And I slept more than was normal for me.

I would lie on my back, meditating for hours on end and visualizing energy going from one part of the bone across the break to the other part. Then, as I would drift off to sleep, I would put into motion the scientific manifestation process and repeatedly played my movie. In my mind, I saw the scene of me being in front of the surgeon as he's looking at the X-ray and saying, "I don't know how this is possible, but it's healed." I felt the feelings of being powerful, relieved, and strong in my body.

Six weeks later, this is exactly what happened. We saw on the X-ray that my collarbone had fused perfectly, and that shoulder is now stronger than the one that was reconstructed. And another bonus—I did this within three months and was in tip-top shape for the start of ski season!

Navigating the Bureaucracy

While in Central America on a speaking tour where I was teaching entrepreneurs about Intentionality and specifically about the components of the scientific manifestation process, I recognized that there was one major problem. I wasn't practicing what I was preaching. My American business visa, the document that would allow me to continue working in the U.S., had lapsed. And along with the pandemic came the closure of most visa offices that provided this documentation. In fact, that wasn't just in America. Nobody was accepting foreign nationals—and on top of that, it was impossible for me to get back into Australia because of the travel restrictions. So, along with a long line of other people in similar positions, I was stateless.

I'd been stressing and avoiding the situation for over a year. I was able to stay in the U.S. as a tourist, but each time I reentered, I was getting questioned more and more about my intentions. With my speaking career, I was traveling quite regularly, and one time, while coming back from an event in Ecuador, I was detained for nine hours in Texas and they threatened never to let me in the country again. After this, I knew I needed to try a new approach. This is when I turned to the scientific manifestation process.

I first felt the feelings of freedom, of being able to work and travel without the constant anxiety of threat. I felt the feelings of celebration, how good it was that I obtained a visa. And I felt awe: awe over the fact that against the odds and circumstances, I can do anything I put my mind to. I then imagined a scene where I left the consulate to call my partner on FaceTime, and she saw me holding up my visa. I proclaimed, "Got the visa!" Her response was, "I knew it!" And we both smiled and laughed in celebration.

As I did this manifestation repeatedly for a few days in a row, I began getting some insights and ideas for actions I could take. My subconscious sent me a message to reach out to the Mexico City consulate (I had been in a different consulate system in Mexico, but I had no idea of when an appointment would become available or whether their systems had crossover), just in case anything had changed in their review process. Within 24 hours, I got an e-mail response. They were receiving applications and would take a transfer. I sent them all of my paperwork immediately, and a few weeks later, I received an e-mail saying they needed more information. Now, this wasn't bad news, but it wasn't good either.

I reflected on this request, on what I'd learned about progress rarely moving in a straight line. Part of scientific manifestation is acknowledging that when things aren't going smoothly, you've got to start taking an inventory of what else could be contributing factors. So I had to consider whether there were any outstanding negative energies or unresolved issues around my visa process.

I assessed where any low vibrations might be in my process, and I realized that my relationship with my attorneys hadn't been very amicable. I had been negative with them, and I was hung up on my perception that they hadn't been doing a good job. We weren't communicating well with one another, and I ended every conversation feeling frustrated and helpless. I decided to reach out and ask for a phone call to clear the air, and to their credit, we had a call that same day, a Sunday evening. I took ownership of my experiences and feelings and shared that with them. They took some ownership, and we were able to move forward. I also let them know that I wanted to strategize all possible ways that we could make this visa happen.

When the call was over, I had a renewed love for my lawyers, and I was feeling really positive about our relationship. Now, nothing happened that night. It was Sunday and offices weren't open. However, on Monday morning, I saw an e-mail come through from the consulate saying, "Mr. Kelly, are you available to come to our offices next week for an immediate interview for your E-2 visa? One spot has become available." I have no idea how this happened, but these were the words I'd been waiting to hear for two-plus years!

Now, this is where the miracle happens. You don't need to fully understand how or why. You just need to accept and allow the manifestation—the miracle you've made—to unfold.

So that's exactly what I did. I was amazed by the power of intention. I saw that as I healed the negativity in my situation, things immediately started to change. I accepted the interview and flew to Mexico City the very next day. A few days later, I was at my appointment and I got the visa!

I hadn't been allowed to take my phone into the consulate building, so when I returned to the hotel, I expected to find my partner there anxiously waiting. However, she was not there, so I picked up the phone and made the call I'd rehearsed in my mind so diligently over the last month. The only difference between my manifestation work and what actually happened is that I didn't get the visa on the day of the appointment; that takes a little more time. So I held up the receipt and in the same vein said, "Got the visa!"

And in response, my partner said, "I knew it!"

It was incredible!

There were so many different things that had to happen to make my manifestation come to fruition. I had to keep believing and stay with the process, even when my senses and the physical evidence were telling me otherwise and were tempting me to believe that what I wanted was impossible.

I had to remain connected to my desired feelings and not fall back into my negative belief loops. I knew that I had already created my reality and just had to wait for it to come from the energetic field into matter. And I had to be patient and trust the universe.

I was diligent. I was disciplined. I was determined. These are all behaviors within reach for everyone willing to use this accelerant.

CHAPTER 15

MAKING YOUR MIRACLES

Because scientific manifestation is such a critical component of the Intentionality journey, I want to share with you a few client stories that highlight how impactful the process has been and continues to be for anyone ready to make their miracle!

Property Power

Two clients (who are also friends) were staying with my partner and me over a recent Christmas break. Early in their visit, I noticed that whenever any conversation came up about the future, there was an awkwardness. This couple owned a property that, for many logistical and financial reasons, weighed heavily on both of them and, as a result, on their relationship.

Every time they tried to discuss any decisions about their future, there was a blockage in their communication, and as the property market kept softening, they lost more confidence that they could get what they wanted for their home. I asked them if they were willing to try the scientific manifestation process, as I was confident it would work in their circumstance. But first we had to explore the ways in which they might have been contributing to their current situation.

Together, we first *clarified* what they wanted—to sell their property with ease and to get a certain amount of money, which would enable them to buy a new property and also have some financial freedom. I then asked, "If you had that, what would you feel?" And they said they would feel freedom, happiness, and abundance. We then dropped into a meditation where I asked, "If you already knew you'd sold the property, what would you do?"

And they said, "We know exactly what we'd do. There's a place along the beach with a great view. We would walk there, pour a glass of champagne, and toast each other. We would say, 'We are free!'" They both were aligned in their vision and excitement, so we then moved to the conception phase.

For the next few nights, they followed the *conception* process— dropping into a meditation before going to sleep, connecting to all the abundance they already had in their lives to raise their vibration, and then playing their movie scene. They continued doing so after they returned home; I had instructed them to do this every night until something happened within them—like a bolt of energy coming through, a subtle shift in perception, or a deep knowing. What's interesting is that this shift didn't have to occur simultaneously for them. He felt it one week later, and she didn't have her full confidence until some time after. Yet regardless, their manifestation was in action.

A few weeks after that, they sent me a message detailing what they'd done upon returning home as part of the *claim* phase of their manifestation. They behaved in ways that were indicative the property had sold, including looking for their next property and getting their financial documents in order. They started to do little acts of pushing the sale, like reaching out more regularly to the broker and being more creative with ways the property could be positioned for sale. More and more, the inspirations came to them. After a month, they had sold the property for more than they'd initially identified in our process together!

So they did exactly what they said they would do—they walked down the beach, toasted with their favorite champagne, and savored their newfound freedom. I got an amazing photo of them at sunset where they are glowing with happiness. In less than six weeks, they had transitioned from stories of why they couldn't sell the house and why their dreams needed to be delayed to unburdening themselves and manifesting their dream scenario.

Truth Be Told

Last year a client of mine who is in the medical profession was traveling and during a holiday party began feeling unwell. She had a headache and a variety of mild symptoms so she accepted some medicine offered to her by an acquaintance. It seemed like no big deal. She knew the people she was with. She believed that what was being given to her was from a trusted source. This was unfortunately not the case.

Her symptoms worsened, and her condition declined. She finally agreed to go to the emergency room, where a battery of tests were run. The substances in her system were illegal and highly dangerous. Concerned that she wasn't telling the truth and that the presence of these substances was a violation of her terms of employment as a member of the healthcare system, the emergency physician reported her to his superiors. She was quickly labeled as a possible drug addict, at sudden risk of having her medical license revoked, and forced to enroll in an intensive rehabilitation program with frequent testing and monitoring. The program was located halfway across the country from where she lived, and she was treated like a prisoner: no visitors were allowed, she had limited phone time at the end of each day, and she was only able to leave once she cleared the strict protocols.

The program was designed for people with addictions—and she had been grouped in with a number of people navigating alcohol, pornography, and heroin addictions, among other things. One prerequisite for leaving the program and keeping her medical license was that she had to pass a lie detector test where she was asked about the substances. But she failed the test after she honestly answered that she had, in fact, ingested (albeit without her knowledge) the illegal substances in question.

A polygraph is often criticized as "junk science"[1] and an outdated, reductive method for correlating physiological trends in the human body with intention and truthfulness. So it made sense to respond with a science-based approach. We started with recoding and identified her belief that she wasn't worthy. We worked to create a positive belief loop about worthiness, and she learned the paths for repetition. Then, with the intention of successfully passing the lie detector test, we began the scientific manifestation process.

First, we *clarified* what she ultimately wanted—which was to be let out of the unwarranted supervision and to feel liberated. Then we discussed what would happen if she was able to pass the test and leave the institution. She saw herself seeing the positive test results and saying to herself, "I did it! It's finally over." Then she visualized flying home, walking through the door of her house, and being welcomed by her husband and child, feeling the warmth and connection of being back together.

We then went through the *conception* phase. She saw herself taking the test, passing it, and packing her bags. She played this out for a few nights and noticed an immediate shift into a more peaceful and calm state. When it was time for her to *claim* her reality and take the lie-detector test, she was completely confident. She believed she'd already passed the test, and because of this, she regulated her breathing and became superrelaxed. She knew that she hadn't knowingly taken the illegal substance and that she wasn't lying. So she continued to breathe through it and feel her truth, and ultimately she passed the test and returned to her family, feeling relieved that this was finally behind her.

With the scientific manifestation process, she was able to, in the present moment, change her reality. Effectively, she recreated the past in the present moment so that it was as if she had never taken that substance. Then her subconscious followed suit.

Due Process

Another client of mine was in a legal battle. He was an elite athlete and had been working with a business partner on developing a health product he thought would revolutionize the industry. Right before the launch date, miscommunications among the partners got to a tipping point and everything imploded. The business partnership went south and resulted in a legal battle that had been dragging on for over a year. At this point my client and his wife were expecting their first child and the ongoing monthly expense of the legal costs, in addition to the emotional toll it was taking on them, was unsustainable. He was burned out and exhausted and seemingly at capacity all the time. He couldn't comprehend how he could keep managing all this on top of the responsibility of a newborn.

He was in too deep to just walk away, and while the financial outcome was definitely a component, he more so wanted to be warranted for all the time, energy, and passion he had invested into the business venture.

Together we *clarified* what feelings he would have knowing that the case was closed and he had been awarded the compensation. He said he would feel vindicated, resolved, and joyful.

Next, I asked him to describe a movie scene that would symbolize that outcome. He pictured seeing his lawyer's name pop up on his phone screen, pressing the Answer button, and hearing the lawyer say, "It's done, and the money's in the bank." He would then look at his wife and give her a big smile as she gave a big cheer.

For the next week, they both participated in the *conception* of their manifestation and played this movie scene out in their minds. This might remind you of the couple manifesting their dream property and have you wondering if you can do a joint manifestation. The answer is yes—you can tag team on your manifestations! This process is even more powerful when working in tandem with your spouse, business partner, child, and so on.

Two months later my client was at home with his now very pregnant wife when his phone started to vibrate, and he saw it was his lawyer calling. He knew this was his moment to *claim*, the final step of the process—he hit the green button, and those magic words came through the phone speaker: "It's done. The money's in the bank." He turned to his wife, and she let out a cheer as they celebrated the news. They felt overjoyed at the birth of this manifestation and ready for their next little miracle that was due in just three weeks' time.

Whether you're navigating a work crisis, trying to unburden yourself from a longstanding weight hanging over your head, or pursuing a lifelong dream, the scientific manifestation process can be an accelerant for the smallest to the biggest ultimate outcomes in your life.

CONCLUSION

Choosing Your Path

So much of Intentionality is about embracing the opportunity to interpret the information available to you and then intuiting the best possible path forward.

What I've shared is a series of paths that hopefully offer you actionable insights into what's possible when you create a life of intention. All allusions to teachers, thinkers, and dreamers I admire, and to scientific and spiritual texts that have impacted me, are simply meant to be signposts that may inspire you in one direction or another.

But there is no single path. There is no one exact way. And if you ever find yourself being sold the story that there is, be wary: the gains from a quick fix are often short-lived. Because the sobering—and thrilling—truth remains: you are your own miracle maker.

And being your own miracle maker means your path can be paved only by you.

It means that it is only you who can truly interrogate the complex codings of your system, ignite the extraordinary transformation available to you with recoding, and take the quantum leaps that can be made with the scientific manifestation process.

It is only you who can create your own inner peace.

It is only you who can prioritize your feelings, knowing that when you surrender to your true nature, you can dance with divinity and co-create with her.

And it is only you who can acknowledge and act on the radical, transformative reality that you are always just one breath away from Intentionality.

*To become more conscious
is the greatest gift
anyone can give to the world;
moreover, in a ripple effect,
the gift comes back to its source.*

— DR. DAVID HAWKINS

ENDNOTES

INTRODUCTION

1. Carl Sagan, *The Demon-Haunted World* (New York: Ballantine Books, 1997), 29.

CHAPTER I

1. "Scientific Foundation of the HeartMath System," HeartMath Institute, https://www.heartmath.org/science/.

CHAPTER 2

1. Lupien et al., "Effects of Stress throughout the Lifespan on the Brain, Behaviour and Cognition," *Nature Reviews Neuroscience* 10, no. 6 (April 29, 2009): 434–45, https://doi.org/10.1038/nrn2639. Quoted in: Hon. Margaret Norrie McCain, J. Fraser Mustard, and Kerry McCuaig, "The Limbic System Pathways," Early Childhood Education Report, 2011, https://ecereport.ca/en/early-years-studies/early-years-study-3-2011/chapter-2-early-life-and-learning-behaviour-and-health/4-limbic-system-pathways/.

2. Charil et al., "Prenatal Stress and Brain Development," *Brain Research Reviews* 65, no. 1 (October 2010): 56–79, https://doi.org/10.1016/j.brainresrev.2010.06.002. Quoted in McCain, Early Childhood Education Report.

3. Bruce Lipton, *The Biology of Belief* (Carlsbad, CA: Hay House, 2016).

4. Craig Gustafson, "Bruce Lipton, PhD: The Jump from Cell Culture to Consciousness," *Integrative Medicine* 16, no. 6 (December 2017): 44–50, https://www.ncbi.nlm.nih.gov/pmc/articles/PMC6438088/.

5. Bigthinkeditor, "Max Planck: 'I Regard Consciousness as Fundamental . . .'," Big Think, December 22, 2014, https://bigthink.com/words-of-wisdom/max-planck-i-regard-consciousness-as-fundamental/.

CHAPTER 4

1. Victoria Esposito, "Plate-Spinning: A Vaudeville Essential," The American Vaudeville Museum, n.d., The University of Arizona, https://vaudeville.sites.arizona.edu/2023/03/28/plate-spinning-a-vaudeville-essential-by-victoria-esposito/.

2. Dr. David Hawkins, "Dr. David Hawkins: How to Let Go of the Past." YouTube video, March 16, 2021, https://www.youtube.com/watch?v=HqwEx_0l0VI.

CHAPTER 5

1. Robert Herrick, *Hesperides: Or, The Works Both Humane and Divine of Robert Herrick, Volume 29*, (Boston, MA: Houghton, Mifflin, 1889), 66.

2. Alexandra Bruell, "How Zumba Built a Brand with a Cult Following in Just a Few Years," *AdAge*, August 20, 2012, https://adage.com/article/cmo-interviews/zumba-built-a-cult-a-years/236737.

3. Bessel A. van der Kolk, "The Body Keeps the Score: Memory and the Evolving Psychobiology of Posttraumatic Stress," *Harvard Review of Psychiatry* 5, no. 1 (Jan-Feb 1994): 253–265. https://doi.org/10.3109/10673229409017088.

4. Bessel A. van der Kolk, *The Body Keeps the Score: Brain, Mind, and Body in the Healing of Trauma* (New York: Penguin Books, 2015), 195–6.

5. Emily Widra and Tiana Herring, "States of Incarceration: The Global Context 2021," September 2021, https://www.prisonpolicy.org/global/2021.html.

6. Dr. David Hawkins, "Dr. David Hawkins: Context vs. Content," YouTube video, shared October 27, 2020, https://www.youtube.com/watch?v=4ebSXU0-QcE.

7. "Dr. Rosemarie Allen: Preschool-to-Prison Pipeline," TedxMileHigh, July 17, 2020, https://www.tedxmilehigh.com/preschool-to-prison-pipeline/.

8. Kadish Morris, "Ocean Vuong: 'I Don't Believe a Writer Should Don't Believe that a Writer Should Just Keep Writing as Long as They're Alive,'" *The Guardian*, June 3, 2023, https://www.theguardian.com/books/2023/jun/03/ocean-vuong-i-dont-believe-writer-should-just-keep-writing-as-long-as-theyre-alive-time-is-a-mother-paperback/.

9. A. C. Shilton, "You Accomplished Something Great. So Now What?" *New York Times*, May 28, 2019, https://www.nytimes.com/2019/05/28/smarter-living/you-accomplished-something-great-so-now-what.html.

10. Shilton, "You Accomplished Something Great. So Now What?"

11. Chris L. Hayes (@chrislhayes), "There's an old saying in newsrooms that 'we don't cover the planes that land,' which is to say the news runs on crisis and disaster and bad things happening unexpectedly and not things slowly getting better, and yet . . . " *X*, June 6, 2023, https://x.com/chrislhayes/status/1666165461711572996?s=20.

12. Quoted in Jonathan Gottschall, *The Story Paradox: How Our Love of Storytelling Builds Societies and Tears Them Down* (New York: Basic Books, 2021).

13. Lisa Feldman Barrett, *How Emotions Are Made: The Secret Life of the Brain* (New York: Mariner Books, 2017), 282–3.

14. Tom Knowles, "I'm So Sorry, Says Inventor of Endless Online Scrolling," *Times (UK)*, April 27, 2019, https://www.thetimes.co.uk/article/i-m-so-sorry-says-inventor-of-endless-online-scrolling-9lrv59mdk.

15. Jessica Klein, "The Darkly Soothing Compulsion of 'Doomscrolling," BBC.com, March 3, 2021, https://www.bbc.com/worklife/article/20210226-the-darkly-soothing-compulsion-of-doomscrolling.

16. Jeremy Goldman, "Airbnb's Focus on Employee and Customer Experience Is Having a Transformative Impact Across a Number of Sectors," Insider Intelligence, July 5, 2022, https://www.insiderintelligence.com/content/airbnb-s-focus-on-employee-customer-experience-having-transformative-impact-across-number-of-sectors.

17. Rebecca Rifkin, "In U.S., 55% of Workers Get Sense of Identity from Their Job," Gallup, August 22, 2014, https://news.gallup.com/poll/175400/workers-sense-identity-job.aspx.

18. Kimberly Lawson, "Why You Should Take Time to Mourn during Career Transitions," *New York Times*, August 23, 2018, https://www.nytimes.com/2018/08/23/smarter-living/why-you-should-take-time-to-mourn-during-career-transitions.html.

19. Barrett, 81.

20. Barrett, 81.

21. Barrett, 81.

22. Gerald L. Clore, Karen Gasper, and Erika Garvin "Affect as Information," in Joseph P. Forgas (ed.), *Handbook of Affect and Social Cognition* (New York: Psychology Press, 2001): 121-14, https://doi.org/10.4324/9781410606181.

23. Gerald L. Clore and Karen Gasper, "Feeling Is Believing: Some Affective Influences on Belief," in N. H. Frijda, A. S. R. Manstead, & S. Bem (eds.), *Emotions and Beliefs: How Do Emotions Influence Beliefs?* (Cambridge: Cambridge University Press, 2000): 10–44.

24. Clore and Gasper, "Feeling Is Believing."

25. Andrew Weil, "Three Breathing Exercises and Techniques," Dr.Weil.com, last reviewed Feb 2022, https://www.drweil.com/health-wellness/body-mind-spirit/stress-anxiety/breathing-three-exercises/.

CHAPTER 6

1. Kari Paul, "Microsoft Japan Tested a Four-Day Work Week and Productivity Jumped by 40%," *The Guardian*, November 4, 2019, https://www.theguardian.com/technology/2019/nov/04/microsoft-japan-four-day-work-week-productivity.

2. Jill Filipovic, "Opinion: Maryland Is Striking a Blow at the Absurd Culture of Over-Work," CNN Opinion, January 31, 2023, https://www.cnn.com /2023/01/31/opinions/maryland-bill-four-day-workweek-filipovic-ctrp /index.html.

3. Arthur C. Brooks, "Meetings Are Miserable," *The Atlantic*, November 17, 2022, https://www.theatlantic.com/family/archive/2022/11/why-meetings -are-terrible-happiness/672144/.

4. Brigham and Women's Hospital, "One in Five Adults Experience Chronic Pain," ScienceDaily, April 20, 2021, https://www.sciencedaily.com /releases/2021/04/210420092901.htm.

5. Jeff Wilser, "The Pandemic of Work-from-Home Injuries," *New York Times*, September 4, 2020, https://www.nytimes.com/2020/09/04/well/live /ergonomics-work-from-home-injuries.html.

6. Gelles et al., "Elon Musk Details 'Excruciating' Personal Toll of Tesla Turmoil," August 16, 2018, https://www.nytimes.com/2018/08/16/business /elon-musk-interview-tesla.html?.

7. Tim Cook (@tim_cook), "Got some extra rest for today's event. Slept in 'til 4:30," X, March 9, 2015, https://x.com/tim_cook/status/574910443413622785.

8. Holly MacCormick, "How Stress Affects Your Brain and How to Reverse It," Stanford Medicine Scope (Beyond the Headlines), October 7, 2020, https:// scopeblog.stanford.edu/2020/10/07/how-stress-affects-your-brain-and-how- to-reverse-it/.

9. Liza J. Severs, Elke Vlemincx, and Jan-Marino Ramirez, "The Psychophysiology of the Sigh: I: The Sigh from the Physiological Perspective," *Biological Physiology* 170 (April 2022): 108313, https://doi.org/10.1016/j.biopsy-cho.2022.108313.

10. Hadley Leggett, "'Cyclic Sighing' Can Help Breathe Away Anxiety," Stanford Medicine Scope (Beyond the Headlines), February 9, 2023, https:// scopeblog.stanford.edu/2023/02/09/cyclic-sighing-can-help-breathe-away- anxiety/.

11. MacCormick, "How Stress Affects Your Brain."

12. MacCormick, "How Stress Affects Your Brain."

13. James Nestor, *Breath: The New Science of a Lost Art* (New York: Riverhead Books, 2020), 221.

14. Kendra Cherry, "What Causes Learned Helplessness?" Verywell Mind, April 11, 2023, https://www.verywellmind.com/what-is-learned-helplessness -2795326.

15. History.com Editors, "Ford Factory Workers Get 40-Hour Week," History .com, last updated April 29, 2020, https://www.history.com/this-day-in -history/ford-factory-workers-get-40-hour-week.

16. Brad Beaven, "The Modern Phenomenon of the Weekend," BBC.com, January 20, 2020, https://www.bbc.com/worklife/article/20200117 -the-modern-phenomenon-of-the-weekend.

17. Dr. David Hawkins, "Dr. David Hawkins: How to Let Go of the Past." YouTube video, shared March 16, 2021, https://www.youtube.com /watch?v=HqwEx_0l0VI.

CHAPTER 7

1. "Sacred Sites," The StarHouse, https://www.thestarhouse.org/sacred-sites.

CHAPTER 10

1. "Science of the Heart: Exploring the Role of the Heart in Human Performance," HeartMath Institute, https://www.heartmath.org/research /science-of-the-heart/heart-brain-communication/.

2. Ali M. Alshami, "Pain: Is It All in the Brain or the Heart?" *Current Pain and Headache Reports* 23, no. 88 (November 2019), https://doi.org/10.1007 /s11916-019-0827-4.

3. Alshami, "Pain."

CHAPTER 15

1. Katrina Gulliver, "Lie Detectors Are Junk Science, but We Keep Using Them," Reason.com, March 2, 2023, https://reason.com/2023/03/07/lie -detectors-are-junk-science-but-we-keep-using-them/.

ACKNOWLEDGMENTS

In the theater of life, every character leaves an indelible mark on the script, and I'm indebted to those who've shared the stage with me in this grand production.

To my spiritual partner, Sydney: Your unwavering belief in me has been the bedrock upon which I've built my courage to unveil my soul to the world. You, gorgeous girl, are the living embodiment of Miss Intentionality, always keeping me grounded and ensuring I never stray too far into the illusion that any of it matters. Thank you for being my self-proclaimed greatest teacher.

And to the unsung heroes behind the scenes, particularly Sam: Enduring a two-year rollercoaster ride with me deserves its own accolade. Your knack for unraveling my tales and weaving them into a cohesive narrative is nothing short of inspirational. And to my partners at Hay House: Lisa, your infectious enthusiasm fueled my writing fervor, and the fact that you came and did the transformative work in our divine feminine immersion was the greatest gift you could give me. Monica, you were the glue that held it all together. Faceout Studio, Jeff Miller, and Karim Garcia, you brought *Intentionality* to life through your beautiful cover art—you crushed it! Allison, thanks for championing me and my book proposal; your positive energy made me know that I had found my people to partner with.

Reid, on our first phone call I appreciated how easily we got to a place of depth. I am not sure what made you quickly form a belief in me; however, it was very humbling and reassuring hearing from your team as we went through the selection process that you were a fan.

Becoming a Hay House author is one of my great miracles, one meticulously crafted through the Scientific Manifestation process. Cassandra, your belief in my vision and the serendipitous introduction set this miraculous journey in motion.

To my breath brother, Shaboomi: In the lonely expanse of service, our connection was a beacon of solace. Thank you for nourishing my body, for seeing me, and for being our children's fairy godmother—truly, a breath bond forged in the ethereal realms.

Dr. Searing, you were a lighthouse in my darkest storms, illuminating my gifts and instilling the courage to embrace the unseen magic that guides our healing journey.

For everyone who has had the courage to join me on their Intentionality path, thank you for your trust and stepping into the unknown. Tracy, your early trust in my abilities remains etched in my heart as a testament to the journey we've shared.

And to my esteemed EO forum, the Cosmic MCs: Brian, Mike, Tariq, Tilio, and Brent—our collective evolution has been nothing short of cosmic, transforming us into better men with each shared revelation.

To my family, the architects of my identity: Your myriad quirks and beliefs have sculpted me into the person I am today, a mosaic of your love and influence.

The Buddha extolled the greatest miracle as the "Miracle of Instruction." This reminds me of the privilege I have of being part of so many people's transformations.

From my heart to your heart.

ABOUT
THE AUTHOR

As a sought-after speaker, event facilitator, and executive coach, **Finnian Kelly** has been dubbed "the Business Mystic" because of his unique ability to put consciousness into business and inspire leaders to find new levels of meaning and purpose through their creative endeavors.

As the creator and chief visionary officer of Intentionality.com, Finnian built and exited two multi-million dollar companies in the financial industry. Through the four paths of his Intentionality framework, Finnian guides people to be purposeful and aligned in their beliefs, thoughts, and behaviors so they can feel more love in their life.

www.intentionality.com

HAY HOUSE TITLES OF RELATED INTEREST

YOU CAN HEAL YOUR LIFE, the movie,
starring Louise Hay & Friends
(available as an online streaming video)
www.hayhouse.com/louise-movie

THE SHIFT, the movie,
starring Dr. Wayne W. Dyer
(available as a an online streaming video)
www.hayhouse.com/the-shift-movie

***

*THE BREATHABLE BODY: Transforming
Your World and Your Life, One Breath
at a Time,* by Robert Litman

*BREATHE HOW YOU WANT TO FEEL: Your Breathing
Tool Kit for Better Health, Restorative Sleep, and
Deeper Connection,* by Matteo Pistono

*THE HIGHEST LEVEL OF ENLIGHTENMENT:
Transcend the Levels of Consciousness for
Total Self-Realization,* by Dr. David Hawkins

*SPIRITUAL ACTIVATOR: 5 Steps to Clearing,
Unblocking, and Protecting Your Energy to Attract
More Love, Joy, and Purpose,* by Oliver Niño

All of the above are available at your local bookstore,
or may be ordered by contacting Hay House (see next page).

***

We hope you enjoyed this Hay House book. If you'd like to receive our online catalog featuring additional information on Hay House books and products, or if you'd like to find out more about the Hay Foundation, please contact:

Hay House LLC, P.O. Box 5100, Carlsbad, CA 92018-5100
(760) 431-7695 or (800) 654-5126
www.hayhouse.com® • www.hayfoundation.org

———

Published in Australia by:
Hay House Australia Publishing Pty Ltd
18/36 Ralph St., Alexandria NSW 2015
Phone: +61 (02) 9669 4299
www.hayhouse.com.au

Published in the United Kingdom by:
Hay House UK Ltd
The Sixth Floor, Watson House,
54 Baker Street, London W1U 7BU
Phone: +44 (0) 203 927 7290
www.hayhouse.co.uk

Published in India by:
Hay House Publishers (India) Pvt Ltd
Muskaan Complex, Plot No. 3,
B-2, Vasant Kunj, New Delhi 110 070
Phone: +91 11 41761620
www.hayhouse.co.in

———

Access New Knowledge.
Anytime. Anywhere.

Learn and evolve at your own pace
with the world's leading experts.

www.hayhouseU.com